Happy 60th Birthday

Love
H Ciani Libby
X

More Memories

of

Croydon

The publishers would like to thank the following companies for their support in the production of this book

Main Sponsor
Minerva Plc

Adams Bros

Cropico

Croydon College

Drummond Centre

Fairfield (Croydon) Limited

Fortidec

Old Palace School of John Whitgift

Raworth Moss and Cook

Rowland Bros

F L Smidth Limited

H Tinsley & Co Limited

Trinity School

Turtles

Whitgift Foundation

Whitgift School

First published in Great Britain by True North Books Limited
England HX5 9AE
01422 377977

ISBN 1 903204 35 6

Text, design and origination by True North Books Limited
Printed and bound by The Amadeus Press Limited

More Memories

of

Croydon

Edited by Stephen Griffiths

Contents

Introduction

You are now well on your way to making your third mistake. The first was to open this book. A second error came along when you began reading. Before too long you will be turning this page and launching into a nostalgic journey that will keep you enthralled until the very last page. You have already been hooked. Be prepared to travel on a magic carpet of recollections as you revisit the town as it was in the last century. This, the latest in the series of thoughtful looks at the past, comes to you as 'More Memories of Croydon'. It is a delightful collection of photographs from days gone by, complemented by stimulating text. Marry these together and you have an excuse to curl up by the fire, lost in a world that time nearly forgot. Thanks to the magic of the camera and the British ability to reminisce, here is a book that tells you how the town looked to your parents and grandparents. Older readers will have personal experience of some of the events captured here forever. It will help settle a few arguments as to where certain buildings stood or when other incidents occurred. 'More Memories of Croydon' may also provoke a few arguments and recriminations.

Grandpa always said that trams stopped running before the war. Now we can prove that his memory is not quite what it was. However, there will be many other instances when he will be able to say, 'I told you so'.

'More Memories of Croydon' is not intended to be a history book. It is not stuffed full of dry facts. Instead it relies as much on the memory banks and nostalgic powers of the reader as it does on its own content. If you are the sort of person who enjoys Opal Fruits, beer in dimpled glasses, vegetables sold by the pound and Ford Prefect motor cars, this is the book for you. Relive the days of royal visits, the street parties and the grand architecture that preceded the high rise office blocks. While you do so remember that not everything in the 20th century was a delight. It brought us two world wars and the carnage of the blitz. There was slum housing and poverty on the streets. Free secondary education was for the middle classes until after the second world war. Medical care for all only arrived with the birth of the National Health Service in the summer of 1948. But, let us be positive. Amidst the difficult times there were many more that were joyous. 'Happy days are here again' in the form of these beautiful, poignant and nostalgic pages.

To understand today we must have knowledge of, or at least insight into, the past. Without that there is no future. We learn from experience and then progress. Croydon has come a long way since first mention was made of it in public records. Development has not been smooth. There are periods of rapid growth followed by plateaux of consolidation. Its ancient origins go back to beyond 5,000 BC. However, the first significant settlements came during Roman times. The Saxons then followed. They established themselves in large numbers around the eighth century AD. The town name was coined from 'Crogdene', probably meaning 'saffron valley'. Saffron is obtained from the crocus plant. It is not too fanciful to imagine fields of the yellow flowers swaying in the breeze. Croydon is mentioned in the Domesday Book of 1086. It already had a church and mill for its 365 inhabitants. Lanfranc, Archbishop of Canterbury, was the lord of the manor. Croydon Manor, where the River Wandle rises at the foot of the chalk hills, was presented by William the Conqueror to Archbishop Lanfranc. His summer residence, the Old Palace, still stands. It was used by successive Archbishops of Canterbury until the mid 18th century. It is now part of a girls' school. After relinquishing the palace, the Archbishops lived nearby at Addington, now the Royal College of Church Music. They left there in 1896. Six Archbishops of Canterbury are buried in Croydon's parish Church of St. John, including John Whitgift. He founded the school and almshouses (1596-99) that bear his name.

In 1276 the town was granted a charter to hold a weekly market. This helped to establish Croydon as an urban centre. It developed into one of Surrey's foremost market towns. It was important for the production of charcoal, the main fuel of medieval times. Newer industries developed during the Tudor period. Tanning, brewing and the production of oatmeal all had some significance. In addition Croydon was a major stopping

place on the London to Brighton road. As the seaside resort increased in fashionable popularity during the Georgian era, Croydon's influence rose as a coaching town. By the beginning of the 19th century it had become the terminus for two new transport links. The horse drawn Surrey Iron Railway opened in 1803, followed by Croydon Canal in 1809. Although both these closed before the middle of the century, trade and population had expanded hand in hand. The opening of the new steam railway in 1839 ensured the continued growth. Croydon's ability to seize the initiative in transport development was repeated in the 20th century. Croydon Aerodrome was established in 1915. It was London's civil airport, only being replaced after World War II by Heathrow. The Victorian town had been a commuter haven for the middle classes who worked in the capital. In 1883 it was incorporated as a borough. This was in keeping with what had become the

largest town in Surrey. Things changed in 1965 with the formation of the Greater London Council. Croydon's 33 square miles were established by amalgamating the former county borough and the adjacent district of Coulsdon and Purley.

The formation of the new borough coincided with the creation of today's skyline. Massive redevelopment took place. Many central London businesses relocated here and huge office blocks and retail centres sprouted, reaching ever skywards. The town took on the look of a mini New York. Roads were widened and remodelled. Multi storey car parks appeared. Traffic swept under and over other highways. Pedestrianised areas and one way systems were designed. Even trams returned to the streets. Now you are prepared for that third mistake you are about to make. You are to enter the land of yesteryear. There is no turning back. Once settled in that armchair you have consigned yourself to a flight into a nostalgic world. It will be the best mistake you have ever made. 'More Memories of Croydon' will act as your personal Tardis. Be prepared to meet butchers in aprons, clippies on buses. Suck on a bullseye or drag on a Woodbine. Walk again along North End, dodging the Hillman Minx and Humber Hawk turning down from Crown Hill. Buy your silks and ribbons at Grant's or walk the expansive frontage that was Kennard's. Look out for bargains in the sales where a tanner has been slashed from the price. Rock to the sound of Marty Wilde's songs as you bop at the Orchid. You were a teenager in love, once over. Get out the sewing pattern and treadle the old Singer. Put on a headscarf and recall that you escaped the worst of the doodlebugs. Go back to a year when we had three kings on the throne. It is all waiting for you.

Street scenes

The trams are running along George Street. 'So what?' you might ask. 'What's new?' In the 2000s Tramlink's smart red and white Viennese cars trundle merrily along the road, clockwise around Croydon. They can reach up to 50 mph, but not within the town. A six car tram can hold 200 people. It is an efficient system of public transport that has returned to a number of towns and cities in the last few years. Manchester, Sheffield and Birmingham have similar systems. Yet, for nearly 50 years, they were missing from our streets. The last ones ran in Croydon in 1951. But for the war they would have been phased out earlier. Trolleybuses, introduced in 1933, had been earmarked as replacements. Horses drew the first trams along Croydon's streets in 1879. Electrification was introduced between 1901 and 1906. Then the town became a mass of overhead cables and pantographs sucking electricity into the tram's power box. The clanking machines were regarded as something typically British. Noisy, draughty and slow, they were somehow loveable. The one making its way towards the camera was the last one to run as part of the Addiscombe tramway service. The town waved it goodbye on 31 March 1927, but reserved its real accolade for 7 April 1951. When the last tram of that era made its farewell journey crowds lined the route from Purley Depot to Thornton Heath. Two horses were put into a mock harness for the last leg of the journey, just to remind passengers of how it all began.

Cobbled streets of granite setts and modern tarmac roads sat side by side at the start of the 1930s. On George Street, for now, old and new transport happily lived side by side. The occasional horse drawn cart might still lumber up the road, but motorised transport had started to make its mark. There were still plenty of cyclists to be seen, for cars were expensive and unreliable. The two wheelers would make a comeback in the 1940s when petrol rationing meant that cars were garaged. Most of the pedestrians on George Street were women. It was daytime and the men went to work. Most women stayed at home to run the house. There were no fridges or freezers, so shopping for fresh food was an exercise carried out several times a week. Wealthier families had a servant or housekeeper to carry out the task. The lady of the house was then free to involve herself in charitable work. Men regarded it as their duty to provide for the little woman and the offspring. This principle crossed the social classes, even if everyone did not accept it. However, it had taken until 1928 for women to gain full voting equality with men. Universal attitudes were not going to change overnight. Most of those out on George Street thought more about what they needed from the shops they were visiting. Each one had its own stamp and style. Shopkeepers knew their customers personally. Shopping was its own social experience in 1930.

Above: The neatly worked balustrade on the top of 70 George Street is an architectural feature that no one would bother to create nowadays. Modern buildings have straight lines, not interesting stone features, cornices and intricately worked decorations. Looking down on George Street, from the corner with Park Lane, the public halls can be seen on the left. For many years they were the main venue for a variety of arts festivals and cultural events. Grand concerts were held there. They became home to the Croydon School of Art and Croydon National History and Scientific Society. The evening rush hour, even as long ago as the 1950s, was a dreadful waste of time. It gave workers a chance to reflect on the day's business. There was little chance of a quick journey home, so those on the top deck of the bus pulled out the crossword. A car is struggling to join the main flow alongside J & T Robinson Ltd. Ogden Smith used to run its business from the shop above Robinson's. It sold keep nets, rods, reels, gaffs and all manner of fishing tackle. Many a good yarn was spun about the one that got away. Most of these buildings went when the road was widened.

Facing page, left: This was the year that the music died. Buddy Holly was a much loved pop singer. In just two years of stardom, backed by the Crickets, he had built up an international following after hits with 'Peggy Sue', 'Oh Boy' and 'That'll be the day'. When he was killed in the plane crash that also took the lives of the Big Bopper (JP Richardson) and Ritchie Valens, a cult was born. His short life even inspired 'Buddy', a hit West End musical in the 1990s. The photographer on the top of a bus at the bridge by East Croydon station was probably whistling 'It doesn't matter any more' as he looked west down George Street. That was Buddy's aptly named posthumous no 1 hit. On 27 May 1959 the Railway Hotel was doing good business. The number of cars parked on the forecourt let us know that the breathalyser and drink driving laws were still

nearly a decade away. The pub served its first pint in 1841. So many hotels and hostelries sprang up around that time as the age of the steam travel came into being. Many of the buildings in this picture were demolished in later times. Even some of their replacements did not make it to the end of the century. Essex House, a large office block built on the left hand side, was one such development to come and go. The NLA Tower, formerly Lowndes Tower, is the most dramatically styled building in this area today. The Railway Hotel lasted longer than most, but even its popularity did not save it. The pub was pulled down in 1980. Yet more offices were built on the site.

Left: The line of cars parked along Katharine Street in early 1954 would not go unmolested today. Traffic wardens would swoop, ready to plaster tickets on windscreens. Denver boots would be clamped to car wheels. Trucks would arrive to tow away the offending vehicle. Motor cars are loved in the 21st century only if you pay through the nose to park them 50 feet up in the air. The town hall stands on the south side of the street, to the right. It is Croydon's third town hall. This one dates from 1896. No one is really sure when the first one was built. Arguments rage as to whether it was 1566 or 1609. Historians are more confident about the arrival of the second town hall. That was in 1808. Alderman Fred Edridge JP, the town mayor, laid the foundation stone for today's building on 9 June 1892. The ceremony was also attended by the town clerk, CM Elborough. Charles Henman designed the impressive building. Gillett and Johnston, who also provided the clock and bells for the stately 176 foot tower, built it. The town hall is part of a complex of Katharine Street buildings that include the 1893 Union Bank chambers and the central library. A statue of Queen Victoria gazes north, under the watchful eye of John Whitgift. His statue is built into the library wall, close to sculpted friezes that proclaim 'health, study, religion, recreation and music'.

Below: The Osborne & Stevens lorry headed the rush hour queue at the George Street traffic lights, ready to cross Park Lane. The bus behind was an express service. That seems to be something of a joke. This was 1956. By the look of the traffic it would be nearly 1957 before it got anywhere. The cyclists had the better idea. It was usually quicker to get around town on two wheels rather than four. The buses waiting in the line were all full of people trying to get home from work. Just think how long it would have taken if they all had cars. The queue would have stretched all the way to Addiscombe. A lonely baby Austin sat in between two of the buses. The driver must have felt quite vulnerable sandwiched in between these two giants of the road. Big red buses were immortalised in a Flanders and Swann song about a 'big six wheeler, diesel engined, 97 horsepower omnibus'. However, passengers did not feel as romantic as that duo about their transport. They just wanted to get home. The hands on John Thrift's clock tower moved more quickly than the traffic waiting below. Thrift was a grocer and provisioner. The company was founded in 1857. It opened for business on Church Street, but moved to George Street when it outgrew its original site. The business was sold to the Edward Paul Company of Camberwell in 1960. Within a few short years the building was demolished.

Right: Taking photographs is not just a case of pointing your Brownie in the right direction. It also demands nerves of steel and a steady hand. On 30 May 1950 this photographer had clambered to the top of Grant's department store on High Street. From there he gazed down along Surrey Street. Shoppers were weaving their way in and out of the market stalls, hoping to find something to eke out the meagre postwar food ration. The cries of the traders echoed in their ears as each one tried to encourage the housewives to part with a mixture of cash and coupons. Stallholders kept a special eye out for their regular customers. They built up good relations with a favoured few. It was a practice dating back over many centuries. Thanks to the power of the church, a charter to hold a weekly market in the town had been granted in 1276. Successive Archbishops of Canterbury, Kilwardby, Stratford and Reynolds, obtained grants by royal charter for the continuation of markets in medieval times. Croydon developed as one of Surrey's main market towns. Grain and livestock were the main commodities traded in those days. At one time the town had a flourishing fish market. Middle Row used to be called Fishmarket Street. In 1314 and 1343 Croydon was given the right to hold two fairs. The main one, Walnut Fair, was held in October. In the early 19th century it was ceremonially opened with a golden key. It was popular for livestock trading, luxury goods and entertainment. The fair ceased to be held at Fairfield in the 1860s, moving to other smaller sites until it folded during the first world war.

The street lamps and shop lights were reflected in the High Street puddles on a rainy evening in 1952. The central light that gleamed brightly over the roadway was removed in 1957. Underneath, the pedestrians making their way over the crossing were indulging in a fairly new experience. They were trying out an addition to road safety. The white rectangles had only recently been painted. Their look gave rise to the nickname that was adopted throughout the country - zebra crossing. The flashing, yellow orbs at the kerbside were introduced in Britain during the late 1930s. Known as Belisha beacons, they owed their name to Leslie Hore-Belisha. He was the minister of transport given the job of overseeing the changes brought about by the Road Traffic Bill of 1934. Plans were made to copy a successful Parisian experiment with pedestrian crossings and the improvement to road safety was launched. The black and white markings on the roadway did not come to Britain until 1951. As shoppers and office workers set off for home, they looked forward to an evening by the fireside. Family life was different 50 years ago. Parents played games with their children. Playing cards were brought out. Little ones joined in for a game of Old Maid or Donkey. Older children were introduced to rummy, canasta and whist. Board games of Monopoly and Scoop were popular ways to while away the hours until bedtime. There was just time for a nourishing cup of Ovaltine or Horlicks before that climb up the little wooden hill.

Above: Postwar rationing was coming to an end in 1954. We had begun to turn the corner from those times of austerity. Looking east along George Street, over the crossroads with Park Lane and Wellesley Road, the traffic was quite light. The age of the family saloon on every driveway was not far away, but it had not dominated the highways just yet. The country had seen great social changes since the war ended. The welfare state had arrived. Free secondary education was provided for everyone. Industries had been nationalised. We had the National Health Service. Despite the innovations and improvements, people still felt that there was not enough in their pay packets. Funding the new visions of the Labour government was expensive. There was also the cost of rebuilding our shattered cities. Voters once again turned to Winston Churchill to lead them into the future. But it took time. Workers were impatient. The old middle classes had taken us into a war, but it was the working man who had to provide the muscle of recovery. Extra pressure on workforces brought predictable results. Dockers in London, Rochester, Hull and Southampton went on strike in protest over compulsory overtime. Even the prime minister had his grumbles. A special painting of him by Graham Sutherland was unveiled. Churchill sarcastically called it a 'remarkable example of modern art'.

Below: There were a couple of adventurous women near the High Street junction with George Street. They had come into town bareheaded. The older ladies did not copy the trend and placed their hats and bonnets firmly on their heads before leaving home. Hemlines, for the modern miss, hovered around calf length. Flat shoes were beginning to give way to those with a stylish heel. The presence of tramlines tell us that the fashion parade was taking place c1950. The buses coming up from North End took full control of public transport on Croydon's streets in 1951. They waited by the Whitgift almshouses that are still home to some elderly residents. Allder's store towers above the traffic. Joshua Allder came to North End in 1862. He opened two shops, side by side, selling linen and silks. He was an astute businessman who recognised the change in Victorian shopping habits. Tradesmen used to visit customers in their homes. If he came into town the shopkeeper would carry purchases to the carriage waiting outside. Gradually, it became acceptable for even genteel customers to enter a shop. The success of the department store followed. As trade increased Joshua Allder bought up neighbouring properties until he had a chain of shops along the east side of North End. He died in 1904, having set the company on the way to becoming the third largest department store in the country.

Below: The raised view takes in most of George Street as it looked c1960. Looking east from the junction with North End and High Street, the road leads towards East Croydon Station. The distinctive clock tower, beyond Wellesley Road, belonged to John Thrift's grocery warehouse. Until 1893 the clock had formed part of Croydon's second town hall. The warehouse and tower, as well as many neighbouring properties, were demolished later in the 1960s as part of the various road improvement schemes. The west part of George Street has retained much of its old character. A collection of insurance companies and building societies use many of the premises, illustrating the growth in the financial sector in recent years. The tall buildings on the left have stood for over a century. The street was then one of the most important shopping areas in Croydon. Included within these buildings is The George, formerly the George Inn. It gave its name to the street. Now part of the JD Wetherspoon chain, it is good to see that the old name has been retained. So often good old pub names are replaced by the Rat and Crowbar, Moon and Mantilla, Termite and Sausage or some other crazy title. The George has had a checkered career. It used to stand opposite the old Whitgift almshouses. An early landlady was supposed to have been responsible for the disappearance of a number of the George's guests. It is said she murdered them in their beds and then chopped their bodies into bite size pieces. She boiled them up in the kitchen, earning herself the nickname 'Old Mother Hotwater'. There is no truth in the rumour that she later opened a burger bar.

Summertime on George Street showed a fine balance between the old and the new. The longstanding three and four storey shops were about to be dwarfed by the modern developments behind. As Bob Dylan put it the following decade, 'The times they were a changing.' Since the Tories regained power, by August 1958 we had our third different prime minister. Harold Macmillan took over the helm in 1957. It was a good time to take over the reins. A mood of confidence filled the air. George Street shops were filled with luxury goods that more and more of us could afford. The streets hummed to the motors of sleek new cars. It was not just the bank manager, doctor or solicitor who had purchasing power. The working classes demanded the attention that their new buying power required. Those working on the factory floor arrived by car as often as they did by bus or bike. Housewives and young women started to buy their fashions at Glazer's, rather than running something up at home from a pattern they had copied from 'Woman's Realm'. Attitudes to money changed. We no longer saved up until we could pay cash for an item. We used hire purchase. So much down and a few bob a week became commonplace. Entertainment altered. Coffee bars for teenagers replaced tea shops. The Everly Brothers superseded Vic Damone in the pop music charts. Jerry Lee Lewis took over from Harry Belafonte.

At leisure

Below left: An elephant never forgets. Nor will the lad who has just dismounted from his bike or the bowler hatted city gent. They were both quite taken with this sight that brought the traffic to a halt in North End on 16 July 1935. It is good to see that the elephant driver, flat hat clamped as firmly on his head as the Woodbine stub between his lips, was watching the traffic lights. They had just changed to amber and six tons of pachyderm trundling across the junction would not

have gone down too well with motorists coming from the other side. The sight of such a creature in the middle of town was not quite as unusual as you might think. Whilst those who had drunk one too many often encountered the pink variety, there were occasions when even the most sober citizen met Nellie or her ancestors. Travelling circuses, such as Sanger's, were regular callers. They set up their big tops in the parks and advertised their presence with a parade through town. Stiltwalkers, clowns and jugglers went along the road, accompanied by the occasional camel, plumed pony or elephant. If Jumbo was part of such a parade, quite what had happened to the rest of the entourage seems to be a mystery. Maybe they had jumped the lights. Whatever the case, there was plenty of nourishment for the allotment rhubarb left on the ground once the lights had changed to green.

Bottom: Looking north along Union Street in 1934 we are reminded that not everyone lived in middle class houses and mini mansions. Surrey folk did not have a monopoly on good living. There were also the terraced homes, often populated by the poorer classes. For this group of women and children life was tough. Mass unemployment led to angry rallies in Hyde Park. Britain was still struggling to pay off its war debt, 16 years after the last bullet had been fired. Dissidents used the situation to stir up trouble. Oswald Mosley launched the British Union of Fascists. There was fighting in the streets and ordinary people wondered where it was all leading to. It was the needs of the family that occupied the minds of the residents of Union Street. Was there enough food to put on the table at teatime? How on earth was mum going to be able to put warm clothing on the children for the rest of the winter? It was only January and she still had several months of shivering ahead. Coal only burned in one grate in the house. The family huddled for warmth in one room before making that chilly march up to bed. At least the children slept two in a bed. They could cuddle up together. When the new day dawned everyone got dressed in front of the embers of last night's fire. If the rent man called they ducked down behind the settee. There was no money for him this week.

In those first couple of years after the second world war we tried to get back to normal. Some of the pleasures denied to us were revived with passion. Huge crowds flocked to soccer and cricket grounds to watch professional sport again. Travel became important once again. Petrol was still heavily rationed, but we had good old steam. British Railways boomed as hordes of trippers went off on holiday or days out. During the summer there were even twice weekly evening excursions to Brighton and Hove. People could do a day's work and still get to the coast for a few hours. The South Norwood Chamber of Commerce had decided to treat itself to a day at the seaside. It put aside the horrid memories of V-2 rocket that killed six people at Sunnybank in October

1944. Its members brought coats, just in case. You can never trust a British summer. Having posed for the photograph they trundled onto the platform and boarded the train. With a snort of steam and a cheery whistle the locomotive pulled them away through the fields towards the salty breezes of the coast. Then it was time to enjoy again a deckchair on the sands. Dad had a knotted hankie ready to protect his head in case the sun shone. Mum daringly hitched her skirt up around her thighs and went for a paddle. Fish and chips in a seafront café, followed by a pint and a sweet sherry in the King George, and they were ready for that last stroll along the prom. The talk at work the next day was all about the great day out, just like it used to be before the war.

At first glance you might think they are on their way to visit an old castle. It is nothing so historic or romantic. Dad and the children were heading towards the water pumping station, off Surrey Street. The sun was shining brightly on 20 July 1951. Britain was hoping to turn the corner from the austerity of the immediate war years. The recently held Festival of Britain offered an opportunity to rejoice. Soon Churchill would return to 10 Downing Street. But the real future lay in the hands of the children enjoying their time with Dad. They were the product of the baby boomer years. In the late 1940s there was an explosion in the birth rate. Servicemen were reunited with their loved ones after the war. Nature took its course. The stork put in for overtime. Looking at this trio who would ever imagine that the children had been born into a world that had allowed 55 million to perish in six years of war? The little lad in his dungarees and his sister in her pretty frock just had to grow up in a better world. Their father tried to help. He spoke of a time when everyone got on together. He told them stories of good people who did away with evil. He led his offspring from the shadows into the bright sunlight of a new dawn. Just to make sure they were on the right path he held their hands firmly, but with the tender loving strength that only a father can show.

Above: Saturday night at the Orchid Ballroom, Purley was when you strutted your stuff. The dance hall opened in 1950 when crooners like Jimmy Young, Vera Lynn, Anne Shelton and Eddie Fisher were popular. The big band sound of Ted Heath and Joe Loss provided the music for us to dance to. It was mainly a time of foxtrots, quicksteps and the waltz. Girls sat at the side of the dance floor and waited for some beau to come across and ask her for the pleasure of the next dance. Everyone knew how to do a spin turn, chassis or lock step. Some of the livelier souls had seen the jitterbug or jive, but if you wanted proper dancing that meant holding your partner as closely as she would allow. Then came Bill Haley and his Comets. The tubby, balding 30 year old lead singer was an unlikely teenagers'

icon. Yet, his 'Shake, rattle and roll' hit the pop charts in 1954. The follow up, 'Rock around the clock', from the film 'Blackboard Jungle', meant that 1955 would see the start of a music revolution that affected modern culture throughout the western world. David Whitfield and Dickie Valentine were out. Little Richard and Gene Vincent were in. These jivers at the Orchid in late 1955 horrified their parents with their noisy music and frenetic dancing. The young man on the right went on to stardom, but not as a dancer. Can you recognise him, perhaps from the ears? He hid his rocking talents in the 1990s when he starred in a stage show about those old maestros Flanagan and Allen. The jiver supreme is that very funny man, Roy Hudd. His cheeky comedy still amuses today's audiences listening to 'Huddlines' on the radio.

Wartime

Below: The women look a little bemused by the air raid shelter on display near their homes. They greeted it with a slight smile and some scratching of the head in the early days of the war. Times and attitudes would soon change. When the blitz began in earnest people were glad of some place of shelter. At first Croydon had been declared a neutral zone with regard to bombing risks. That was soon changed to high risk and some children, even those as young as the toddler here, were evacuated to safer areas. The attacks upon the capital began in earnest in the early autumn of 1940. People were glad that they had their Anderson and Morrison shelters. Those who found them quaint before the bombing began now thanked their lucky stars for their provision. There were all sorts of different ways people found to shelter when the rain of death began. In some towns openings led from the street into underground cellars and crypts. People took refuge in the Tube. Others took their blankets, provisions and candles down the garden to their personal shelter, half buried in the back garden. They tried to keep it as an adventure for the little ones, but the sound of explosions nearby was not easy to explain away. When the all clear went it was with some anxiety that they emerged from their refuges. They did not know what they would find. They might have left their house some hours before, but was it still standing on their return?

COUNTY BOROUGH OF CROYDON.
AIR RAID PRECAUTIONS.
DEMONSTRATION
STEEL SHELTER.

Above: In 1940 Coulsdon and Purley had its own urban district council. It was not officially combined with Croydon until 1965, when the Greater London Council came into being. But, in wartime, council boundaries became fudged as we all pulled together towards the common goal of defending our nation. In total, some 3,000 men were employed in dealing with the aftermath of bombing raids. Half of these were brought in from outside the Croydon area, so vast was the task. This group was part of the Coulsdon and Purley heavy rescue gang. It had plenty to do during late 1940 and the first half of the following year. With just the protection of a tin hat and a gas mask each workman was ready to play his part in attending to the buildings shattered during the blitz. It was difficult and dangerous work. Over 1,100 homes were destroyed. Each one had to be made safe. The gang used its props and timbers to shore up where it could. There was the ever present danger that masonry would crash down upon the men. They had to work carefully in case there were people still trapped. Each brick removed might have triggered an unexploded bomb. Any girder lifted could have revealed a severed limb. It was, at times, dirty and disgusting. At the back of their minds was the thought that the next piece of rubble to be moved might prove to be the last. Despite all that the heavy rescue gang worked on. Like so many others these team members thought of their fellows first and put their own interests second.

Right: Is it a bird? Is it a plane? Is it a twister? On 16 August 1940 they were still not sure. After hostilities broke out in September 1939 there was a period known as the phoney war. For months little seemed to be happening that touched us. Men joined up, telling their loved ones that it would be all over in a matter of weeks. Those views had changed by the summer of 1940. Our forces had been thrown back into the sea at Dunkirk. Aerial attacks on our shipping increased and the Channel Islands fell into enemy hands. These men were part of the Air Raid Precautions (ARP) team who had been put on alert. An attempted invasion of the mainland was on the cards. Operation Sea Lion, Hitler's strategic plan, was likely to be launched any day. An aerial strike force was certain to lead it. These men had taken classes in aircraft recognition. There had been an air raid alert and they craned their necks to try to determine whether the shape overhead was friendly or if it belonged to a Junkers Ju88 or Heinkel H111. The ARP had been around since 1935. Military experts knew that future wars would be determined by air power. They were also aware that civilians could become involved as direct targets. When war was declared the ARP gained many volunteers, offering their services as wardens, firewatchers and plane spotters. This ARP group would have plenty to see in the following weeks as the Battle of Britain raged overhead. Thanks to the skill of our pilots and the support from the ground Operation Sea Lion was abandoned.

Both pages: There is one in every street. It is that chap who always has a project on the go or the one who marks special occasions with his own individual stamp. For one it is gardening. There is a new patio to be laid. There might be a pond to be excavated. Some might want to re-turf the back garden. Others prefer to erect sheds and greenhouses. Then there are the avid DIY addicts. Rooms are knocked through, a bathroom put in or the old kitchen ripped out. We have seen loft conversions and pebble dashing. But, it all needs enthusiasm. Those not interested in all the year round activity save themselves for that special push. When Christmas comes they have the flashiest reindeer hanging from the roof. The fairy lights around the house are reminiscent of an airfield runway. The jolly snowman in the front garden is big enough to frighten the neighbour's children. If that is not enough, there are always coronations and jubilees to be attended to. The largest union flags, the brightest bunting and the finest window tableaux will appear.

So, what was going on at 68 Whitworth Road, South Norwood? Tons of sand had been dumped on the pavement in late 1939. Was the family about to build its own seaside resort, linking Whitehorse Lane and Selhurst Road? Buckets and spades were in evidence, though they did not seem to belong to the sandcastle building variety. There was busy activity in front of the house. Women held sacks open as men shovelled away furiously. In the background the self appointed foreman kept a careful eye on developments. He was the brains behind it all. It was important that he had a vantage point. From there he could survey the scene and determine that all was well. A quiet pull on some thick twist, rammed into his briar by a horny thumb, helped him contemplate calmly. As the sacks were filled and placed in front of the bay window the penny began to drop. A defence line of sandbags began to take shape.

In recent times we have seen the same thing develop as flood barriers. In 2000 and 2001 heavy rains saturated the water table and many homes in lowlying areas were devastated. This was not the case on Whitworth Road. War had been declared just a few months earlier. For the first time civilians were likely to be directly involved in the fighting. In the

late 1930s air raid precautions were taken. Shelters were established. Protection from aerial bombardment was on the minds of those living in built up areas.

After Germany's invasion of Belgium and Poland there was a lull in hostilities. Many thought that peace could still be achieved. Soldiers joined up saying, Back home for Christmas'. Veterans of the first world war knew better. They said the same thing in 1914. Some used this quiet period wisely, building defences and practising rescue skills. This example of sandbagging was one such project.

As the work continued, neighbours joined in to lend a hand. It was one of the features of British life in those days. You mucked in and helped. There was no need to ask for a favour. People just appeared as if you had rubbed a magic bottle. It was an unspoken fact that when one of the helpers started something on his own house others would rally round in return. You could also guarantee that mum would appear at some stage with a welcome cuppa. Then it was time to take the weight off your feet for a while. Our gaffer kept his place above the rest, like some king of the castle. He was not about to surrender pride of place. The happy group enjoyed its refreshment. They were all wreathed in smiles. This period of quiet lulled many into a false sense of security. At the moment it was not much more than a game. The real test was still to come. As the pile of sandbags grew even the co-ordinator had to relinquish his lofty post. There

was a danger that the pile was growing so high that he might be marooned for evermore! He descended to refresh himself with another cup of tea. As he rested his arm on the railing he probably did not realise that the ironwork would disappear before long. It would be requisitioned as part of one of many salvage drives. Anything metallic, from pots and pans to park gates and fences, was collected for recycling. Warships, tanks and aeroplanes were created from what had begun life on the kitchen shelf or ringing a playground.

After a long day's toil the work was done. The mountain of sandbags was in place. The workers departed, tired but happy in a job well done. The women sorted out the evening meal. The children were scrubbed in the bath in front of the fire. The men disappeared to the local for a welcome pint. They had deserved it. As the trio posed in front of the finished product, the whole enterprise began to make more sense. The house was to double as a reporting station for those wanting to do their special bit for the war effort. A couple of little problems remained. How on earth was anyone going to get in through the front door? Then, if that had been managed, how could anyone see a hand in front of his face? Every chink of light had been blocked out. But, don't let such minor details stop us applauding a job well done. We just have to hope that no one was accidentally buried underneath it all.

Below: The Croydon Division of the Civil Defence Corps arrived in South Norwood on 8 October 1955. It was making itself ready for inspection by the mayor. The corps then mounted a display that was to reassure those watching of readiness in the face of civil unrest or hostilities breaking out. It had only been a decade since the final shots had been fired in the war. People were still not confident that a lasting peace had been achieved. They were right to be tense. Since Germany and Japan surrendered there had been trouble in Palestine, the Berlin blockade, the Korean war and revolts in Kenya and Cyprus. Added to these problems was the growing threat of the hydrogen bomb. America, in 1952, and the USSR, in 1953, had both run successful tests. The world was anxious that a holocaust might be unleashed. Civil defence groups mounted practice sessions to show how they would respond in the event of nuclear attack. The Croydon Division often used the derelict building on South Norwood Sewage Farm as a useful focus for their training sessions. This exercise was to show off the Division's state of preparation and its co-operation with other uniformed services, such as the fire and ambulance services. This area is now part of a country park. The modern artificial mound within the park, handy as a viewpoint, was constructed from rubble salvaged from war damaged buildings.

No longer needed, but thanked just the same. This was the last parade and stand down of Croydon's Home Guard in November 1944. To younger readers the Home Guard has become a source of fun. The popular BBC TV series 'Dad's Army' provided many laughs. It showed a bunch of elderly butchers, undertakers and clerks, led by a stuffy bank manager, pretending to be a vital cog in Britain's civil defence. Audiences chuckled at their antics. Although a funny programme, 'Dad's Army' did scant service to the dedication these people displayed in real life. It is true that the force was mainly made up of veterans or those unable to go to the front. But, their willingness to serve and perhaps die in defence of the realm was never in doubt. Admittedly, when initially formed as the Local Defence Volunteers, some of early efforts were ridiculous. One platoon patrolled with imitation rifles once used in a Drury Lane production. Elsewhere catapults were recommended as launching pads for petrol bombs and broomsticks were converted into pikes when knives were attached. The force was renamed the Home Guard in July 1940 and 250,000 men were enrolled. Although still handicapped by a shortage of weapons and resources, they trained with vigour and initiative. If Hitler's forces had crossed the Channel these men would have met them head on. Their equipment might have been limited, but their hearts were as big as footballs. Croydon acknowledged its unsung heroes and packed the streets to thank them by cheering that last parade.

Who can blame the old chap for shedding a tear? As he approached the bomb damage on Cranmer Road he must have wondered when it would all end. He had probably served in the Great War, the conflict that the politicians had said would end all wars. The sacrifices he and his pals had made seemed to have counted for nothing. At least when he was in the trenches his loved ones at home were safe. Now there was no haven from enemy fire. This was not just a one off. The blitz on London and its neighbouring counties began in earnest in 1940. It continued, night after night, for nine months. Only when Germany turned its attention to the invasion of Russia was there any respite. Things seemed to be on the turn in 1944, following the successful D Day landings in June. But, Hitler hit back with a new weapon. The flying bomb or V-1, nicknamed the doodlebug, was launched on Britain. The drone of these pilotless machines, packed with high explosive, brought fear back into the hearts of those living within range of the launch pads on the other side of the Channel. The worst sound was that of silence. When the engine noise stopped, the bomb fell to earth. During the summer of 1944 over 100 doodlebugs were launched against Britain every day. Some 3,000 people were killed. More of these bombs fell on Croydon than any other London Borough. The hit on Cranmer Road took place on 26/27 July. Residents salvaged what few possessions they could, but most were only left with memories.

Events & occasions

Councillor Mrs Roberts had dressed in all her finery for this special occasion. She clutched a small posy that peeked out from the fur muff she carried. The pelt she wore as a stole around her neck further warmed her. Whilst no one would object to the strings of pearls that adorned her neck, imagine the furore from animals' rights groups if the scene were repeated today. Councillor Roberts belonged to an era when animals were meant to be used to fill the bellies and warm the bodies of mankind. She had come to open the new nurses' home on Mayday Road. It is a happy coincidence that the hospital should bear that name, providing help in emergencies as it does. The nurses providing the welcoming party were all turned out in freshly starched uniforms and regulation dark stockings. At night their skirts could be heard crackling and swishing their way down the wards. Historically, women had always been seen as the principal carers for the sick. Certain religious orders in the Middle Ages were established for just that purpose. It was not until the days of Florence Nightingale that nursing became a recognised profession. For most of the 20th century matron oversaw nursing in hospitals. She became a caricature figure, an ogre who ruled her charges with a rod of iron. Doctors trembled in her presence. Trainee nurses fled in terror at her coming. In truth she was the senior nurse who wanted the best for her patients.

The trams clanged their bells. Car drivers tooted horns. Crowds lined the streets and cheered with gusto. Croydon was being afforded the honour of a royal visit. It was no minor royal who came to call on 25 June 1927. The King himself was in town. Three quarters of a century ago there were no televisions to bring us close ups of the royal family. There were newspaper stills, but to see the monarch in the flesh was a treat not to be underrated. The townspeople came in their thousands. George V had arrived to attend the opening ceremony of the first stage of the enlargement of Croydon General Hospital. He was a popular king who had led his subjects though the horrors of the Great War.

Nicknamed 'the sailor king', because of his time in the Royal Navy, he helped endear himself to the nation in 1917. He changed his family name from Saxe Coburg Gotha to Windsor. This went down well as it removed the connection with cousin Kaiser Wilhelm II, leader of the German nation with whom we were at war. The King did not attend many more major functions during the rest of his reign. His health was poor and he declined gradually from the following year until his death in 1936. The flag wavers on the pavement were pleased to have been able to see King George when he was at his best. They liked his bluff frankness and distrust of foreigners. He is reputed to have said, 'I don't like abroad. I've been there once.'

Below: If anyone said that these women were revolting he would have to be very quick to explain what he meant. During the early years of the 20th century women's suffrage was one of the most important political campaigns in the field of human rights. Denied equality, women found a voice and figurehead in Emmeline Pankhurst. She led the revolt against the status quo and male domination. She had already helped to secure limited property and local voting rights in the 19th century. It was her formation of the Women's Social and Political Union in 1903 that provided the big breakthrough. It led to most women being granted the full vote in 1918, complete franchise arriving in 1928. The Great War had seen a further rise in the status of women. They served their country in the field and on the factory floor. They were not to be ignored again. Other movements for change were instituted. This photograph was taken outside Croydon Town Hall on 17 June 1926. It shows peace pilgrims at prayer. Their banners displayed Coulsdon, Purley, Croydon, Tunbridge Wells, Robertsbridge, Hurst Green and Wadhurst as just some of the centres of support their cause had achieved. Despite the 1914-18 war being the one to end all wars, the public was far from convinced. The peace pilgrims were part of a national pressure group that urged the government to take a lead in the disarmament conference at the League of Nations. The protestors were on their way to a large rally in Hyde Park, to be held two days later. 'Law not war' was the motto.

Above: On 9 June 1933 the searchlights from the town hall clocktower cut through the night sky. They shone like a beacon to illuminate the 50th anniversary celebrations of Croydon's incorporation as a borough. Thousands of light bulbs combined to make celebratory arches a glittering display to mark the momentous day. The occasion was marked by a royal visit. Prince George came to town to share in the fun. At the same time he laid a foundation stone for the extension to the General Hospital. During Victorian times Croydon had developed from a haphazard and unhealthy town into one of the most pleasant of areas. Town planners worked hard in providing facilities and a sense of order that had been lacking in the past. Respectable middle class people found it a convenient and comfortable place to live. Croydon's incorporation as a borough in 1883 was a fitting finale to the efforts that had been made. Its elevation to county borough status in 1889 was the icing on the cake. It gave the council even greater powers. Further improvement schemes were undertaken in the 1890s. High Street was widened and, in 1896, a new town hall and clocktower was built in Katharine Street. It became the centrepiece of these jubilee celebrations. Locals were glad to party. This was still the time of the depression when good cheer was in short supply. The golden jubilee came as a welcome distraction.

Locals came out in force on 9 June 1933. They were on Katharine Street celebrating the golden jubilee of Croydon's incorporation as a borough. The Kings Arms, facing the town hall, had once looked out towards High Street. It was pulled down in 1866 to make way for an approach to the Central Railway Station, now the site of the town hall. The Kings Arms was first mentioned in records in 1674. Locals used to draw water from the pump in its yard. The pub was demolished in 1963. Quite a few glasses were raised there, 30 years earlier, as the motorcade swept east along the road. The bells in the clock tower rang a melodious peal. They did justice to the craft of Gillett and Johnston who supplied them nearly 40 years previously. The company is still going strong in South Croydon. Royal standards and union flags were everywhere. Men tossed their hats in the air. Women and children waved little flags. They were in the presence of royalty. The future King of England had come to honour the celebrations. He did not know that he was the future monarch, as he was only second in line to the throne. The abdication of his elder brother in 1936 provided him with the crown. Those lining the streets were not too bothered about the future monarchy. They had come to show pride in their town and loyalty to the House of Windsor.

Above: Mrs Randall wore her crown proudly. She was one of the main organisers of the party being held in St Jude's Church Hall, Thornton Road. The place was packed out as old and young alike had a whale of a time. The youngsters dressed up as the king and queen took pride of place at the table. They looked a little puzzled by all the fuss, but the grownups made up for that with their own merrymaking. The hall had been decked out with streamers, decorations and flags to celebrate the coronation of George VI on 12 May 1937. Children donned their party hats and games of charades, pin the tail on the donkey, blind man's buff and musical chairs were played with great gusto. Some tots played too vigorously and all that jelly and ice cream did not react too well to being shaken about. Still, what is a good do without someone disgracing himself? Adults do it, so why not the youngsters? It was a fun day that had been a long time coming. The king's father had died 16 months previously. In the meantime there had been the proclamation of Edward VIII and his abdication just before Christmas. Albert, Duke of York, the old king's second son, was hurriedly thrust into the limelight. He assumed the throne as George VI with a certain amount of trepidation. He was nervous in public. Fortunately, he had a strong wife to support him and the loyalty of the nation to see him through.

Below: The anti aircraft searchlight beam played across the face of the clocktower on Croydon Town Hall on 6 February 1937. The world was preparing to explode again. Mussolini and Hitler had sent enough warning signs across the Channel that peace in Europe was a fragile commodity. Italy had forged an alliance with Germany just months previously. The Spaniards were engaged in a bloody civil war. Only the ostrich could not see what was coming. Across Britain civil defence groups prepared as best they could. They were handicapped by official attitudes, led by prime minister Chamberlain, that war could be averted. Others knew different. This demonstration by a battalion of the Royal Engineers was part of Croydon's Peace Week. It was a strange mixture of hope for peace and preparation for the inevitable. In less than three years this searchlight, manned by the 315th Croydon Company, would be in action for real. It would track the Luftwaffe bombers across the night sky, trying to light up a target for the ack ack gunners below. The illuminated tower is still one of the town's most notable architectural features. Built of red brick and Portland stone in 1896, Charles Henman's design has survived for over a century. It is just tall enough to be picked out on the skyline as you approach the town. Its attractive dome and spire make a pleasing contrast with the high rise glass and steel around it.

Below: There were 18 adults taking part in these Victory in Europe (VE) celebrations on 8 May 1945. Only five of them were male. That should tell you something about the loss suffered by families in wartime. Some of the missing men would return from the battlefront, though, as there was still the war in the Far East to be concluded. Even so, there would be a permanently empty place at the dinner table in thousands of homes. Nor could the six lost years of normal family life be recaptured. Many of the youngsters about to tuck into the jelly and buns in front of them would hardly know the man who would walk through the door in months to come. The people in the photograph put those thoughts to one side on VE Day. The best gingham cloth was thrown across the table. They sang 'We'll meet again' and 'White cliffs of Dover', whilst hoping that the world really could be free for little Jimmy to sleep in his own room again. The children at the party will be thinking about drawing their pensions by now. Do they still remember the day when Britain went mad for the first time since 1939? Can they recall the hokey cokey they danced, the whistles they blew or the confetti they threw? Or do they still shed a quiet tear for the father who never came back, the grandpa their own children were denied?

Bottom: The trestle tables were borrowed from church halls and school dining rooms. Benches were similarly acquired. Union flags and jolly bunting fluttered from windows and were draped in chains from the lampposts. Streets were closed off and everyone prepared to celebrate. The scene was repeated up and down the land as the nation rejoiced that the war in Europe was over. Six long years of death and destruction had ended. The residents of Lansdowne Road, Purley celebrated in style. VE Day was an occasion that would never be forgotten. On 8 May 1945 all the drabness and deprivation of the war years were forgotten in a blaze of floodlights, fireworks and festivities. Cries of 'God save the king' echoed though the land. Mums spent their week's rations in providing a party spread. The smell of cakes in the oven, the sight of freshly cut sandwiches and the jugs

of homemade lemonade were treats that had been denied to us for so long. There was dancing in the street and passing bobbies were kissed enthusiastically. However, this picture reminds us that not everything in the garden was rosy. The frame is full of children, women and the elderly. There are very few young men in view. So many of them were still in uniform, away in some foreign land. Not all of them would return. Some of those getting ready for the VE party already knew that they had been widowed or that a son was not coming back. They hid their grief to join in with the national celebrations.

Right: It was a sad day for the nation. Croydon played its part in the country's day of grief. A respectful crowd of several thousand gathered near the war memorial outside the town hall on Katharine Street. The bus and the traffic behind came to a standstill as two minutes' silence was begun. All the men in the crowd doffed their hats and the women bowed their heads. You could have heard a pin drop. This was 15 February 1952. At this very moment King George VI was being laid to rest in the vault of his ancestors at St George's Chapel, Windsor. As the coffin left Westminster Hall, where it had lain since his death nine days earlier, the Household Cavalry walked in slow time alongside the gun carriage that acted as a hearse. Three queens were in mourning. The king's mother, Mary of Teck, his wife, the former Elizabeth Bowes-Lyon, and his daughter, the newly proclaimed Elizabeth II. Big Ben chimed 56 times, one for each of the years of so short

a life. In Croydon there were mixed emotions. We were saddened by the loss of our monarch, but his passing heralded a new era. A young and vibrant Queen was on the throne. The last time that had happened saw the Great being put back into Britain. We hoped that Elizabeth would lead the way to prosperity, as her great great grandmother had done 115 years before.

GOD SAVE OUR QUEEN

Bottom left: Little terraced houses shared one thing with large company offices in May 1953. They were decked with flags and bunting ready to celebrate Coronation Day. The decorations on the Gas Offices on Park Lane had a bigger display than we had at home, but the message was the same. We feted our new monarch. When the great day came streets were closed off. Church halls and schoolrooms were raided for their furniture. Trestle tables were dragged out into the roadway. Plates of sandwiches, freshly baked buns, jolly jellies and jugs of lemonade covered the table tops. Children dressed up like little kings and queens. Wind up gramophones were cranked to blare out hokey cokey music. Long congas were danced on the cobblestones. On 2 June it dawned damp and cloudy. That was a minor irritation. Nothing was going to get in the way of our enjoyment. The coronation of Queen Elizabeth II was an event that lived with us forever. The gold coach took her at walking pace past thousands of her cheering subjects to Westminster Abbey. Other heads of state took their places in the procession. Queen Salote of Tonga was one of the most memorable figures. Her huge and beaming frame waved wildly from an open carriage rapidly filling with rain. For many at home it was their first glimpse of an event on television. Nearly 1,000,000 TV sets were sold in the preceding weeks. Families gathered around the little, flickering black and white picture. They listened to the superb tones of Richard Dimbleby's voice describing the pageantry of it all.

Above: Welcome to citizenship. This group of mainly 21 year olds was being given its own key of the door to the new Croydon. This emerging breed of young people had been part of the late 1950s revolution that spawned the word 'teenager'. They were no longer satisfied with being children or even youngsters. They had their own culture and, more importantly, purchasing power. Young men's hairstyles moved away from the old short back and sides. Brylcreem provided a slick look. The more adventurous sported a Tony Curtis style of wave. Suits, collar and tie were still important fashion and formal occasion apparel. Women favoured bright cardigans and woolly tops. These young people were also better educated than their parents were. The 1944 Education Act had provided classless opportunities. Now they were ready to show their muscle. Having become adults at 21, not 18 as it is today, they were mature and experienced enough to realise that the future of Croydon was in their hands. They would be the ones, during the 1960s, to transform the model into life. The redevelopment of the town had begun in 1954 with then widening of George Street. However, it was the Croydon Corporation Act of 1956 that empowered the local authority to buy and develop land. London was encouraging businesses to decentralise and move to the suburbs. The model being examined by these young adults would soon come to life. By the end of 1969, 3.5 million square feet of office space would cover Croydon. There would be 45 blocks in the centre alone. The older men in the photograph had the design, but it was these young men and women who put it into practice.

From Small Beginnings

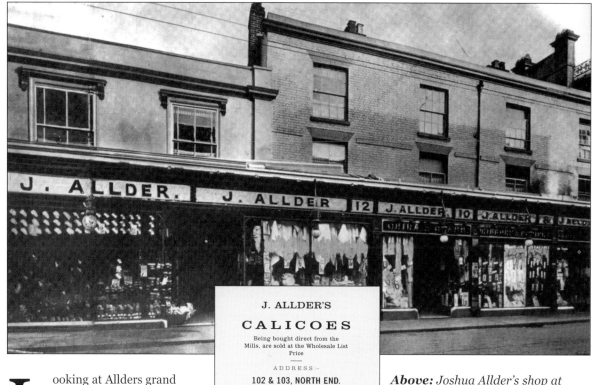

J. ALLDER'S

CALICOES

Being bought direct from the
Mills, are sold at the Wholesale List
Price

ADDRESS:-

102 & 103, NORTH END.

CROYDON

J. ALLDER,

102 103, NORTH END, CROYDON.

BEGS very respectfully to inform his Patrons that
he continues to CLOSE on WEDNESDAY at
FIVE o'clock; on other evenings at EIGHT o'clock
(Saturday excepted)

L ooking at Allders grand property today, with its entrances from North End, George Street, Dingwall Avenue and the Whitgift Centre, it is difficult to believe that this giant grew from very small beginnings.

Above: Joshua Allder's shop at 102/103 North End.
Left: An early advertisement from 1867.
Below: 102/103 is shown in dark grey.

It was in 1862 that Joshua Allder, aged 24, set up his first shop at 102/103 North End. Although the street numbering changed later in the 19th century the original shop was clearly identified on the Ordnance Survey map of 1868.

The relationship between retailer and customer has been a constant process of change and, just as today, the customers of the 1870s sought standards of service and choice that fitted their lifestyles.

Joshua Allder had rightly anticipated a change in the way that fashionwear was sold with a move away from specialist tradesmen visiting the homes of their customers to the new vogue where customers combined the time needed for separate purchases by visiting the retailer. It was within these new department stores that all the items needed by customers were displayed under one roof.

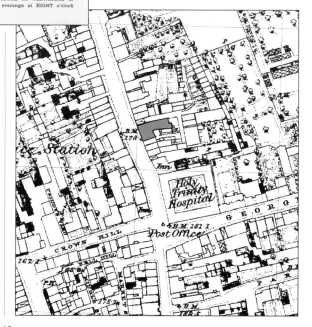

Clearly this change was to the great advantage of the customers for more space was soon required and Joshua was able to add 104,106 and 107 North End, opening specialised departments expanding from fashionwear to linen, drapery, household furnishings and carpets sales. However negotiations to purchase 105 from a long established baker held up his plans, and it was with considerable relief that Joshua was able to complete the jigsaw and carry out the building conversion works that were proudly announced in the Croydon Advertiser in 1886.

During the long wait to acquire the baker's shop Joshua had been active planning his next step. Between his expanding empire and the historic Almshouse lay the Ship Inn, a coaching stop with medieval origins as old as the Almshouses.

Below: *North End in 1885 before Mr Allder's expansion.*
Left centre: *Allders expansion confirmed in an advertisement from 1886.*
Above Left: *The expanded store at 102 to 107 North End shown coloured dark grey.*

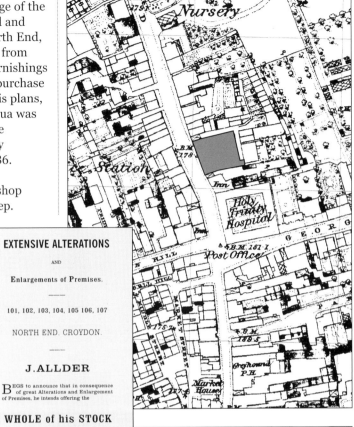

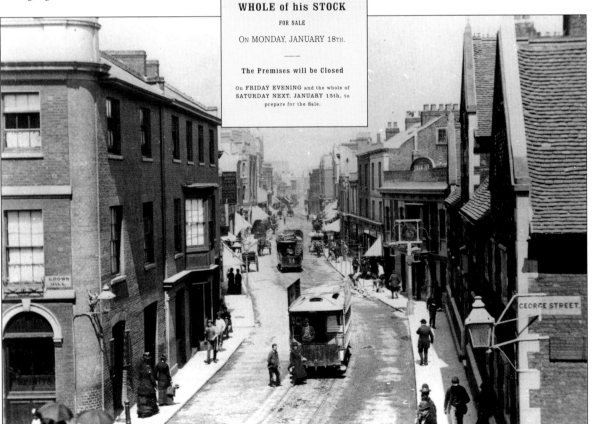

EXTENSIVE ALTERATIONS

AND

Enlargements of Premises.

101, 102, 103, 104, 105 106, 107

NORTH END. CROYDON.

J. ALLDER

BEGS to announce that in consequence of great Alterations and Enlargement of Premises, he intends offering the

WHOLE of his STOCK

FOR SALE

ON MONDAY, JANUARY 18TH.

The Premises will be Closed

On FRIDAY EVENING and the whole of SATURDAY NEXT, JANUARY 15th, to prepare for the Sale.

The role of the coaching inns had declined with improved speed of transport and in time Joshua was able to add the site of the Swan to his store with demolition of the Inn proceeding in 1889 and the emergence by 1894 of the first purpose built department store section of Allders.

The importance of the new department store section of Allders (the renumbered 2/4 North End) compared with the original premises can clearly be seen in the drawing above. By this stage the site of Joshua Allder's store was the same size as the Almshouse, much larger than the original buildings, but tiny compared with the modern store.

Above: *The new building from a drawing of 1894.*
Right: *The expanded store on the Ordnance Survey map of 1896.*

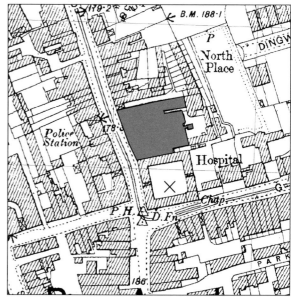

This photograph of 1908 indicates how the replacement for the Swan Inn dominates the other buildings in North End, including Mr Allder's original premises beyond, from which he continued to trade.

The success of the new section that replaced the Swan was sufficient to drive further expansion, but not in North End. Reorganisation on the site of the original Whitgift School permitted the release of the site of the Schoolmaster's House around 1890, and Joshua Allder commissioned the fine Italianate white terracotta building of 1897, the façade of which remains today above the arcade into George St.

The rivalry between Croydon's other department store, Kennards established in 1853, and Allders was always keen. In the 1890s spurred on by Joshua Allder's development of the Swan Inn 'Mr William' and 'Mr Arthur', the sons of the founder, initiated Kennard's expansion.

Their enlarged site, facing Allders in North End, became far more impressive when it was redeveloped with a new purpose built retail store where Kennards were able to boast an impressive frontage with an arcaded window display, some

50 feet deep and running the entire length of the site. It was the construction of Kennards large purpose built store that set the scene for the Allders store we know today.

Above: North End in 1908 after Mr Allder's expansion.
Below Left: The new George St premises of 1897.
Below Right: This map of 1914 shows the expansion into George Street but there is still no sign of today's familiar arcade.

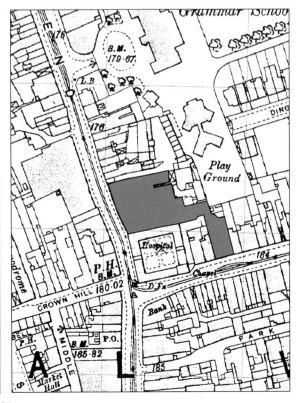

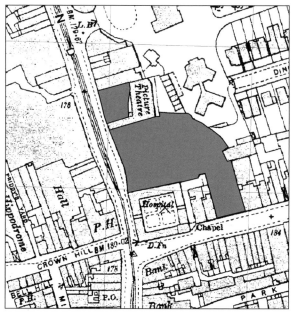

Following the death of Joshua Allder his family sold the business in 1908 to Mr JW Holdron and Mr F C Bearman. They recognised the need to consolidate the various buildings that Joshua had acquired, and to build a grand building.

As with the baker in earlier years, the Scala Theatre stood in the way of their expansion along North End. Having agreed to take 20/30 they could not permit the Scala to sit in the centre of their new frontage. The answer lay in re-housing the Scala towards the rear of the site, but with a fine entrance to the street.

This allowed the construction of the North End frontage that we see today, completed in 1926 and designed to incorporate the first arcade.

Above: *North End after the works of 1926.*
Below Right: *This Ordnance Survey map of 1935 shows the new mall.*

The rebuilding of the store incorporated a small internal arcade, which proved very popular. Recognising the advantage of providing a covered route to help the passage of potential customers saw a revision to the arcade in the early 30's.

Reproduced above and left are parts of the agents letting particulars from 1932. It is interesting to note that they state that 'Shopping under cover has long proved a great attraction', foretelling Croydon's current covered malls by more than 50 years.

A newly designed mall linking North End with George Street was to offer

FOREWORD

CROYDON may well be described as one of the great towns of England. Although only at an average distance of ten miles from London this County Borough provides everything required for its POPULATION of some 234,000 people, to say nothing of the neighbouring districts of Wallington, Sutton, Purley, Coulsdon, Sanderstead, Selsdon, West Wickham and even Beckenham in Kent.

AS A SHOPPING CENTRE its principal stores may well be compared with those of the West End, and the throngs of shoppers who daily pour into the town give ample testimony of its importance in this direction.

THE HEART OF THE SHOPPING AREA is concentrated around the inter-section of the four main trading thoroughfares, viz.—North End, George Street, High Street and Crown Hill.

MESSRS. ALLDERS' STORE is placed in the heart with extensive frontages to North End and George Street, and the making of the Arcade to link these two thoroughfares is an enormously important step in the development of the central shopping area.

SHOPPERS AND PEDESTRIANS will undoubtedly use the Arcade exclusively when proceeding from North End to George Street and vice versa, the congested state of the footpath under the walls of the old Whitgift Hospital being a source of inconvenience.

SHOPPING UNDER COVER has long proved a great attraction, and the window display which Messrs. Allders will have on the South and West side of the Arcade will, in itself, be a great draw to the new pedestrian thoroughfare.

THE PLAN ATTACHED to these particulars clearly shows the importance of the position and the shops which are available.

small kiosks for other traders, improving the choice for customers and helping to further establish the popularity of the enlarged store. With so much shopfront now in Allders' control the next stages of expansion had become obvious.

The continuing need for expansion saw Allders taking over the auditorium of the Scala in 1952 and with minimum changes to the building this opened as the new hardware and gift department.

In 1953 Mr John Lawrence took over the company as Managing Director, and set about plans to capitalise on the excellent frontage that the store possessed with new larger open-plan floors. Sadly the pressure of death duties led to Allders being sold to UDS in 1958 before these plans could be implemented.

Above: *Estate agents details of 1932 show the new mall.*
Left: *The details confirm Croydon's importance to the shoppers of south London.*

The 60s saw strong growth in the size of the store. Inevitably more pieces were added to the jigsaw to achieve this. In February 1960 Allders purchased the business and the premises of the House of Savage, adding both a furniture business and 7a/9 George Street.

Bovis were appointed builders to redevelop the former Scala portion and by August 1960 the Croydon Advertiser was able to report that the plan 'which will make the North End store half as big again as it is at present, is well up to schedule'.

This rebuilding and expansion between North End and Dingwall Avenue created the anchor store for the Whitgift Centre, which was constructed following the Allders expansion.

Following the completion of the Whitgift Centre, which saw a new basement service yard for Allders, it was possible to re-plan the store to swallow up the historic goods yard reached from Dingwall Avenue. Thus in the mid 1970s much of the site towards George Street, last comprehensively developed in the late 19th century, was rebuilt and 220,000 sq.ft of newly built space added. This proved to be a challenge with trade continuing in the North End and Whitgift Centre portions until completion in 1976.

In the years since that major scheme the concentration has largely been to internal refurbishment and

alteration to meet the changing demands of the customers. In 1987 20,000 sq.ft was added with the addition of new retail and restaurant facilities.

Several changes in the management of Allders culminated in a management buy-out in 1989 to form Allders Limited, followed by a successful flotation on the London Stock Exchange in 1993.

1994 saw changes to the Whitgift Centre section with a major overhaul of the important ground floor perfumery hall, and 1999 saw the opening of Act 3, contemporary accommodation on the third floor to house young women's fashions.

Above Left and Right: *Whilst the frontage appeared unaltered from the 1950's much of the store formed a building site throughout the early 1960's.* ***Below:*** *The site of the store as we know it today.*

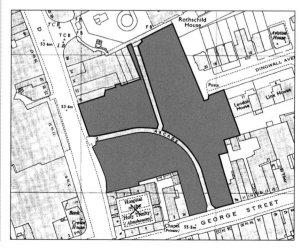

As the 20th century drew to a close changes in department store retailing throughout the country caused the new management team to recognise the need to create a retail environment to match the best elsewhere.

Whereas the evolution of Allders in past years had guaranteed that the store offered the best shopping within Croydon, the current challenge must give Croydon shoppers the standards visible in various locations in central London, in the improved suburban centres of Kingston and Bromley and at the out-of-town destinations of Lakeside and Bluewater.

In order to offer a full range to continuing customers, and without building works disrupting the high standards of service that customers seek, Allders have agreed terms to take a new purpose built store. This will be built south of the existing location, with four large new floors offering clear visibility and easy navigation by customers.

The new Allders store will be the anchor to the Park Place development. The four level store will connect to a wide mall at three levels, above and beneath George Street.

Following completion of the first stage to the south of George Street, and relocation by Allders, all of the

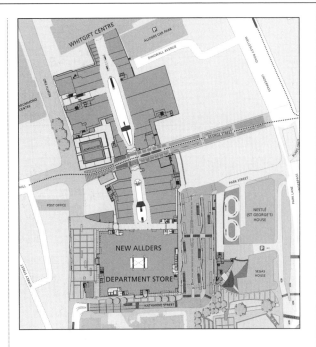

current Allders store north of George Street will be redeveloped as an extension of that three storey mall, connecting to both levels of the Whitgift Centre.

Above Right: *The development plan for Park Place, with the new Allders store as anchor.*
Below: *The new 'Allders Square' - a great place for meeting and entertainment.*

Birds eye view

The 1924 aerial view, northwest of the town centre, shows Mayday Hospital as the focal point of the photograph. There have been long debates about the origin of the hospital's name. It is an appropriate choice. The international distress call of 'Mayday' comes from the French. M'aidez means 'help me'. Its translation into its English form became recognised the world over. Unfortunately, the term's connection with the hospital is pure fancy, however attractive the thought might be. It is simply named after the road on which it was built. Mayday Road has little in common with France. It is more likely to have been given its name after a special event that took place here one May Day. Either that or perhaps people used to dance round a maypole that once stood here. Mayday Road was formerly just a short path, near Bensham House. Maybe it was the place of springtime festivities. The hospital had only just been renamed when this photograph was taken. Until 1923 it had been known as the Union Infirmary, established on 16 May 1885 as one of the Poor Law establishments. The Archbishop of Canterbury attended the opening ceremony in a building that was then set in open grounds that were once part of the Manor of Bensham. Poor Law hospitals were often little more than dumping grounds for the unfortunate, but Mayday Hospital became a proper place of healing.

The outpatients' department at Croydon General Hospital opened in 1925. The Archbishop of Canterbury performed the ceremony. A previous archbishop had opened the 30 bed hospital on its Oakfield Lodge site on London Road in 1873. It had moved there from its original 14 bed place at Duppas Hill. This aerial view was taken to mark the occasion when George V visited two years later on completion of the initial stage of the enlargement of the hospital. It was a sunny day in June. The occupants on the top deck of the tram would have enjoyed the experience, though it was a less attractive perch in wet weather! Talk amongst the passengers was still about the exploits of the American aviator Charles Lindbergh. The previous month he had landed at Le Bourget following the first ever non stop solo flight across the Atlantic. Almost immediately afterwards he flew to Croydon, where a vast crowd turned out to see him. Sports fans were full of golfing news from Massachusetts. The inaugural Ryder Cup competition was in progress. Ted Ray's team was no match for the home side, led by the great Walter Hagen. At home, the King left Croydon to greet the return of his son Albert, Duke of York. He was returning from a royal trip down under. Four days after this picture was taken people craned their necks to catch sight of the first full solar eclipse for 200 years. Fortunately for the hospital outpatients' department it was a cloudy day. There were no cases of eye damage to deal with. The hospital continued to serve the town until its closure in 1996.

There was a time when the Croydon skyline was not dominated by car parks and office blocks. Some of the older monuments and buildings have been preserved. They are still there, if you look hard enough in between the glass, steel and concrete. The water tower at Park Hill was given Grade II listing in 1970. It also boasts a heritage plaque to mark its significance. It was erected in 1867. It is a fine example of Victorian architecture that was attractive, distinctive and still practical. The tower was built to improve the water supply to the higher parts of town, especially the Park Hill estate. Part of the turret was damaged during World War II, but was later repaired. This 1928 aerial view shows a peaceful and almost rural scene. The motor car has yet to clog up the roads. Motoring in those days was much more leisurely than the stress laden chore it has now become. Open topped tourers glided past the elegant mansions. The drivers were dressed in greatcoats, goggles and caps, looking like some form of grounded Biggles. A white scarf usually billowed out behind. A good run out to Epsom, Leatherhead and Box Hill was a popular jaunt for a Sunday. A well stocked hamper, a pretty girl and the open road. What could be better?

Necks craned as people looked up at the plane flying overhead. Even though Croydon Airport had become a busy terminus by 1933 most of us had no experience of air travel. To see an aircraft up above always prompted a look. The skies would be thick with jousting planes during the following decade. Dogfights took place amongst the clouds and bomber planes made their daily assault on the capital. No such thoughts entered our minds as the little plane droned away that peaceful day. True, a funny little man with a silly moustache had just become the German Chancellor. But such an odd looking character could hold no threat to our nation, could he? The cameraman took his aerial shot to mark the 50th anniversary of Croydon's incorporation as a borough. He concentrated in capturing the heart of town. High Street runs up the centre of the picture. It forks right at the junction with Surrey Street, before heading off towards Crown Hill and North End. The town hall on Katharine Street stands out clearly on the right. Even 70 years ago Croydon was a built up area. It had become a popular part of commuter land. Any aerial view taken today would have to take in the high rise developments of the last 30 years. Road layouts have changed, with the flyover cutting across the bottom part of this scene.

On the move

Pedestrians still take their lives into their hands nipping in front of trams running through the town centre. The chap narrowly avoiding the no 42 to Thornton Heath also had lorries and cars to contend with in the late 1940s. Looking down North End from High Street we can see people scurrying like little ants. There was hardly an inch of pavement to be seen. Shoppers spilled into the roadway in their anxiety to get to the next shop on their list. They were keen to make sure their money was wisely spent. There was little spare cash for luxuries. Money was tight in the first few years after the war. Even if we had something to spare, goods were not always available. Rationing bit hard.

Housewives had to eke out food and clothing coupons as best they could. First up in the morning was often best dressed. Some muttered that they wondered just who had won the war. There seemed scant reward for all the sacrifices they had made. The government had controls placed on the manufacture of all manner of goods. Cutlery, jewellery, fertilisers, confectionery and bottling equipment were amongst those that were under restriction. The Morris motor company unveiled its new Minor and two Wolseley models, but who had the petrol to put in their tanks? Mums got out their sewing machines and ran up their own frocks. Dads went off to the allotment and grew extra vegetables for the dinner table.

Below: Now then, now then. What's all this 'ere? It seems a funny place to park up. Perhaps the rider just wanted to jump the queue for the January sales. The sergeant surveying the scene seems unimpressed with that excuse. Was the glum looking chap to the right the rider? It is hard to tell. He is sporting leather gloves, but a motorcyclist would have been more likely to wear gauntlets to keep out the cold on 28 January 1936. Bikers did wear normal clothing when they were out and about. The all over leathers and luminous jackets were several decades away. In the 1930s motor cycle sidecars were popular vehicles. They continued to be a familiar sight on our roads well after the war. Even the AA and RAC used them to bob about our roads, searching for motorists in trouble. However, they were notoriously dangerous. The protection offered to the side car passenger was minimal. Fortunately, not too much damage seems to have been

caused in this accident on London Road. The bike's registration plate, beginning YU, perhaps should have read 'Why me?' as the bobby stood on guard. He had his cape draped over his arm, ready for a rainy squall. But, it was a boring task. He had not earned his stripes to stand around on the pavement. There were more important matters to be considered on that day. The funeral of King George V was taking place at the very same time this picture was taken.

Bottom: This pair of cheerful chappies could help transform your sitting room. They were the delivery men from Stockwell & Oxford on North End, bringing G plan furniture to your doorstep. Fashions determined that tables and chairs became more than just functional. They had to have lines and styles pleasing to the eye. A chair was not something that you just sat on. It was a statement of taste. The delivery men did not mind. Changing fads kept them busy. As the second half of the last century unfolded young couples did away with the fuddy duddy styles beloved by their parents. Laura Ashley prints decorated the windows. Habitat lamps lit up the Dralon chairs. Sepia was abandoned in favour of subtle pastel shades. The world became a brighter place and our homes reflected the freshness of the mood. When Stockwell & Oxford began its operation on North End in 1891 it sold bedsteads and carpets, before extending its range to other furnishing. Seth Oxford and Jesse Stockwell had the sort of Christian names that spoke volumes in the Victorian era. Good, strong, Biblical names gave the impression of reliability. Seth was one of the sons of Adam and Eve. Jesse was the father of King David. How could the firm go wrong? The Oxford family took over the whole business in 1945. The company later moved to Katharine Street. In the 1990s a family member, Seth Oxford's great great grandson, was still running the business.

Below: There was a constant stream of traffic running down towards Church Street from Crown Hill. The morning of 1 June 1957 dawned warm and bright, but the drivers had little chance to enjoy the weather. They were cooped up in their cabs in yet another crawl that blighted driving in town. The old Hippodrome building is in the centre of the picture. British Home Stores had taken it over the previous year. Yet another traditional entertainment centre had fallen by the wayside. It had opened as far back as 1867. In those days it was known as the Theatre Royal. In 1895 it was renamed the Theatre Royal Variety. Top music hall acts provided hours of enjoyment for Croydon audiences. There were singers, dancers and comedians. The variety bill always included speciality acts. Performing seals and dogs jumping through hoops were always popular. There was usually a magician or mindreader, as well as an acrobat and juggler. Variety really was the spice of theatrical life. The theatre became Croydon Hippodrome in 1912 and was turned into a picture palace. The silver screen brought new stars to the town. Rudolph Valentino's sultry looks smouldered in the 1921 film 'The Sheikh'.

Women swooned in their seats at the sight of him. The Hippodrome gained further fame in 1929. It was the first provincial cinema to show talkies. By then Valentino had gone. He died in 1926 at the tender age of 31. His female fans were distraught, though their boyfriends failed to share their grief.

Facing page, top: Brighton Road has its share of pubs along the road from London to the coast. The Swan and Sugar Loaf and the Red Deer are just two of the best known to spring to mind. In days gone by they offered refreshment to travellers using true horse power to get around. The late 1950s found the energy under the bonnet. We had more in our pay packets, more in our pockets. It was part of Macmillan's 'never had it so good' era. Consumer spending rocketed. Electrical appliances, once regarded as luxuries, became commonplace. But nowhere was the boom more marked than in car ownership. Once the prerogative of the middle classes, now most families had their own saloons. The vast majority were British makes or built in factories over here, such as Dagenham and Halewood. The baby

Left: As little children we used to ask the bus conductor for the end of his ticket roll. If he was in a good mood you got the prize. We played games with the numbers on the tickets. Adding up the digits gave a result that could be decoded. A total of 12 meant that you were going to get a kiss from Muriel Humphries. Making 13 was better still. That translated as not getting a kiss from that swot with the National Health glasses. Female conductresses, known as clippies, were popular. Older lads chatted them up. Younger ones could be cheeky with them. They did not give you a thick ear like their male counterparts. The first crafty drag on a Park Drive took place on the top deck. That was usually followed by the first real tinge of green about the gills. In this picture the 68 bus to South Croydon made its way along North End on the afternoon of 6 February 1958. For once there was a hush on the top deck. Word was starting to come through of a plane crash in Germany. The details were unclear, but someone said that Manchester United's soccer team was involved. Only later that evening did confirmation come through. Seven of the country's top players lay dead in Munich. An eighth, Duncan Edwards, died later. Today it is the done thing to vilify the success of that soccer club, but in 1958 everyone loved the Busby Babes. Grown men wept when they heard the terrible news.

Austin, Ford Anglia and Jaguar pictured were all assembled in this country. That put money back into production and the nation prospered. Contrast the scene with the 21st century. Now it is Nissan, Mazda, Renault, BMW and Peugeot that sit on the driveway. It had been Austin, Morris and Singer that held 75 per cent of the market in between the wars. The Rootes group, based on the Hillman and Humber cars, grew in influence in the 1950s. In 1952 Morris and Austin combined as the British Motor Corporation (BMC). The popularity of home produced cars was enhanced by the introduction of the BMC Mini in 1959. The roads might have been congested, but they were filled with the fruits of British engineering.

Shopping spree

Remember the halfpenny? We used to have 480 of them in a pound. In the days of shillings and pence it was a humble coin, but it was worth twice as much as a farthing. This view of George Street, with the old Thrift warehouse and clock tower to the right, is taken from a postcard. With just a halfpenny stamp in place this scene and a jolly message could be on its way to any part of the country. And what a scene it was! Early motor cars and vans jostled for space on the road with horse drawn cabs and carts. Little two wheeled buggies were popular for private use. Their close neighbours, hansom cabs, were widely used as taxis. Pedestrians thronged the pavement and spilled into the street. Cables ran overhead, ready to spark into life as a tramcar approached. Ladies in long, flowing dresses and little boys in Eton collars wandered under the shop awnings. George Street was once the premier shopping street in Croydon. Butchers hung game outside their shops. The smell of newly baked bread wafted past our nostrils. There were little tea shops where ladies could meet and gossip about the latest events in their social whirl. Men had their moustaches waxed in the barber's shop. High class milliners had fine hats on display, including the latest Paris fashions. The middle classes had their own private accounts with dressmakers. Off the peg clothing was not for them. Everything was made to measure.

Above: The Times Furnishing Company was holding a sale. There were great bargains to be had. It was a case of everything must go. Church Street, as seen from Crown Hill, is one of Croydon's oldest. But, development had no thought for history, even in 1930. The steady increase in traffic meant that some widening had to take place around Crown Hill. Those shops that were to be affected had to save what they could from the enforced closures. This was good news for shoppers. Unfortunately, what was a buyer's market also depended upon having cash in your pocket. The country was in a period of depression. In America, the Wall Street stock exchange crashed. The nosedive of 1929 had repercussions the world over. Unemployment in Britain rose and some workers had their wages cut. The chap making his way towards the camera looks prosperous enough. He looks natty in the popular three piece suit of the era. But, who knows what he carried in the package under his arm. Was it all his worldly goods? The woman behind him wore a typical hat of that time. Its bell shape, known as a cloche, had a rim that was pulled down almost to eye level. Skirt lengths crept higher and higher, a far cry from the floor length gowns of her Edwardian mother. Soon, the fashions of the Hollywood stars would make their impact on British women.

Right: Some things do not change. The Oxo logo on the side of the Carter Paterson van is still instantly recognisable. The humble stock cube even inspired a series of TV adverts that ran for ages in the later years of the last century. The story almost became a soap opera. Viewers watched Katy producing marvellous meals for her family. They were conjured up from uninspiring ingredients, a throwback to postwar austerity. However, with Katy's skill and the magical input of Oxo, a meal fit for a king was served up. As the years went by we watched her family grow, whilst all the time marvelling at what she could produce with the addition of a crumbled cube. Eventually, as stable married couples with nice children became unfashionable on TV, they were eased out. Food adverts are now more likely to show single parents or lads being laddish. In this view of 49-53 Church Street in the late 1940s it was still mum who did the shopping. All of these women clutched tight to their handbags and shopping bags. They were the ones who had to make the housekeeping stretch as far as it could. They were well used to doing so. During the war, while hubby was away on foreign fields, they had done everything. Now it was peacetime, but the war had not really been won. Britain was still battling against shortages. Inside the women's bags were ration books. Coupons for fresh meat, fruit, chocolate and clothing were eked out so that the family could be clothed and fed. The clothes that these women wore were practical. There was little money or enough coupons to waste on frippery.

The market on Surrey Street was doing a brisk trade c1935. The stalls stayed open until 9 pm. Late in the day was a good time to hunt for a bargain. By then prices had been cut, especially for fresh produce. Customers knew that the goods had to be sold or they would perish and become worthless. The haggling that took place was conducted with a mixture of good humour and keen business sense. It was a long day for the traders. By the time the last sale had been made many of them had vocal cords that throbbed painfully. It is no wonder that they developed rasping voices. The only way to attract custom was to bellow louder or offer more amusing banter than the competitor next door. Oil lamps lit the market during evening shopping sessions. An acrid smell and thin pall of smoke marked the scene. During the war blackout restrictions meant that the market had to close by 6 pm. Surrey Street market, still busy today, is the only true survivor of the host of markets that once flourished in the town. The decline began in mid Victorian times. Croydon was once described as a great corn market. Grain was traded on the ground floor of the 1809 town hall. A butter market was held until 1874. Other markets were held at Westow Street and Portland Road. The cattle market ran until 1935. The naming of Drovers' Road marks its existence. Surrey Street market was established in its present form in 1922. It is a delightful example of old ways existing alongside the new.

Left: North End was packed with people shopping on this day in the late 1940s. It was mainly women's work. Even after their efforts on the home front during the war, most women happily slipped back into the role of the housewife. The burning of bras and equality in the workplace was 20 years away. Men still regarded it as their duty to provide for the little woman. They were embarrassed by their lack of earning power if she had to look for a job. Even if she found one it was referred to as earning pin money. It was as though the extra money was only really needed for luxuries or female frippery. It must have been a warm day on North End. Young women had put on their short sleeved blouses and done away with their raincoats, confident of a nice day ahead. Two of them stopped to look in Courlander's shop window. Was one of them eyeing up an engagement ring that she might persuade her boyfriend to buy? She could bring him for a walk past here tomorrow and drop a few hints. The hairdresser's on the first floor above offered Marcel waving. A visit up there would provide this pair with a smart perm or wave to show off at Saturday's dance. A call at Edmonds' Wools next door would provide the materials with which to knit a bright new jumper for a beau. All women knew how to knit and sew. Times change. When did you last darn a pair of socks?

Below: The tramlines and overhead cables would soon disappear from North End. By the late 1940s their day was nearly done. The face of this part of the town has been changed significantly since those days. The Whitgift and Drummond Centres now attract the modern shopper off the street and into the complexes inside. North End's wide expanse has been closed to traffic for some time. Pedestrians can stroll freely along the once busy highway, though this photograph shows that petrol rationing was still keeping cars in their garages. In the middle of the last century shoppers were out in force on the pavements. Durbin & McBryde was a chemist's that also dealt in photographic supplies. George Fletcher, the tailor, faced fierce competition from the giant next door. Even so, he could still make a living. Bespoke tailoring had not yet completely given way to the ready to wear market. Marks and Spencer had taken root on most main streets in our towns. It became established as one of the most reliable clothing and food stores for quality and good value. Its own brand name, St Michael, was the guarantee of money well spent. The company began life in 1884 as a stall in an open market in Leeds. Then known as Marks' Penny Bazaar, it was the household goods, haberdashery, toy and sheet music business of Michael Marks, a Jewish refugee from Poland. His sign read, 'Don't ask the price; it's a penny.' In 1894 he took on Thomas Spencer as a business partner. Marks' son, Simon, started the St. Michael brand name and transformed the business from outdoor stalls in various markets of northern England to a chain of indoor shops.

Right: The face of the town changed dramatically in the late 1950s and 1960s. Out with the old, in with the new. Croydon's version of Sylvester Stallone, the demolition man, appeared everywhere. Through the gates a man in a white shirt gazed at the latest example of the remodelling of the town. On 2 July 1958 he was watching the building of Norfolk House. Older readers might just remember him. Jack Pomper was the owner of J & T Robinson at 51 George Street. It was a well established firm that had enjoyed the boom in the sale of electrical appliances. Housewives who had laboured over the dolly tub and mangle gave thanks for the electric washing machine. Soon it became standard equipment in the kitchen. Washday red hands became things of the past. The days of the cold larder were numbered because the price of fridges came within the reach of ordinary families. Carpets were no longer hung on lines and beaten silly. Upright and cylinder vacuum cleaners helped take even more drudgery out of housework. Home entertainment became more varied. Most lounges had a black

and white television screen flickering in the corner. We even had two channels to watch, following the launch of ITV in 1955. Lovers of radio's 'The Archers' paid a price for that. Grace Archer was killed off on ITV's first night in an effort to keep people listening rather than watching. Robinson's did not survive the march of progress. It was demolished as part of the town centre improvements.

Facing page, bottom: Not a car in sight on a quiet day in 1938. The shops were open, but the streets were deserted. Perhaps some were inside Robinson's electrical store, watching the second half of the FA Cup Final on a newfangled television. They would have been among the privileged few to see George Mutch knock in the solitary goal that won the cup for Preston against Huddersfield. If the photographer stood here today his lens would be full of bumper to bumper cars, hordes of people scurrying along their way and banks of traffic lights and road signs. The junction of George Street and Wellesley Court Road has changed beyond all recognition. Bus only lanes and roads closed to traffic were not in the planner's minds before the war. There was room for pedestrians and motorists to live side by side. Within 20 years that had changed. The area became a bottleneck. Roads were remodelled and this section of George Street marooned from its western section. The attractive Thrift's clock tower was one of the later victims of the developers' hammer. A number of buildings on either side of the road were pulled down as a sacrifice to the god of progress. Anyone emerging from the underpass or battling his way along the dual carriageway in the 21st century might argue about the level of improvement to traffic flow.

Top: North End was ablaze with light. It was coming up to Christmas time in the late 1950s.

The fairy lights shone on the conifers. The roof had been cleared for Santa's reindeer to land. In later years the old man came by helicopter, dropping from the sky without the need of Prancer, Dancer and the rest. Inside the store was a magical land of gnomes, pixies and angels. There were animals, pony rides and a miniature zoo. They led the way to that corner of wonder, Father Christmas' grotto. The old man sat, surrounded by powdered snow, sack at the ready as he greeted children with a 'Ho ho ho'. Parents smiled delightedly as he asked each visitor if he had been good. Mum slipped a shilling to one of Santa's little helpers and a present appeared from the pile behind him. They were days of pink for a girl, blue for a boy. The boys got a plastic trumpet or toy drum. That went down well with dad at 4 am on Christmas morning. Girls received a dolly or a magic painting book. You only had to dip a brush in water, apply it to the page and colouring appeared on the figures drawn there. The result was soggy and runny, but it was real magic. Kennards once dominated North End. William Kennard opened a small double fronted shop here in 1852. His influence extended as, by 1895, the store stretched over the old police station. In 1905 further development took place in the opposite direction long North End. By 1933 its arcade windows took up over half a mile of frontage. Kennards eventually became part of the Debenham group.

Croydon's shoppers had taken to the streets in their thousands. Allders was full to bursting. What had been two little shops near the Swan Inn in 1862 had grown into a mammoth department store. It was the first building in the town to have a glass thermal air curtain doorway and also led the way with the first escalator. Through the years it kept pace with the times. But, how styles change. Hemlines go up and down. Trousers narrow and widen again. There are turnups one year and not the next. Hair lengths go from crewcut to shoulder length and back to skinhead. In the early 1970s it was the turn of the flared trouser. Barbers went into liquidation as men grew their hair onto their shoulders. Older folk muttered about Mary Ellens, but young people have seldom given much consideration to what parents thought about the way they looked. Young women sported hot pants. Older men stopped protesting about modern fashion when that form of attire became popular. There was a lot of peeking over the top of newspapers when a long legged 'dolly bird' went by. It was not very good for male blood pressure, but life would be dull without a little danger. The word 'unisex' appeared in our vocabulary. It was a time to say 'peace' and stuff a daffodil into a soldier's gun barrel. In America there were huge protests against the Vietnam War. We had our own troubles at home. Problems in Ireland escalated. In January 1972 British troops shot 13 dead on 'Bloody Sunday' when a civil rights march turned into a riot.

At work

The 1920s were hard times. The war debt from the 1914-18 conflict crippled economies. The world had been torn apart, but rebuilding it was far from easy. In Germany the currency became so devalued that people pushed piles of worthless notes around in wheelbarrows. Britain had major labour problems. Coal miners were threatened with a 13 per cent wage cut. 'Not a penny off the pay, not a minute on the day' was the slogan that roused them to action. The Trades Union Congress supported the stand. It called its members out on a general strike on 5 May 1926. A formal state of emergency was declared as industry ground to a halt. Troops and volunteer workers were used to try to get the country moving. This group of men was employed to keep the Electricity Works operating. It was a difficult choice for them. Other workers thought of them as strike breakers. Their families knew that they were bringing home a wage to keep body and soul together. The balance between poverty and principle was a hard one to strike. The Electricity and Tramways Company paid its staff bonuses to remain in work. The general strike crumbled after nine days, but the point had been made. For most of the remainder of the 20th century the miners would be the ones taking the lead in industrial battles with central government.

Above: This elevated view of Denning Avenue looks across the recreation ground to Duppas Hill and the Waddon housing estate. Waddon Mills are now mainly warehouses and retail outlets. Admiral Lord Horatio Nelson is once supposed to have fished at Waddon Court, though he would not catch more than a cold there these days. The housing estate went up in between the wars. Croydon's busy airport and its excellent road and rail connections with the inner city encouraged the housing boom. It was easy for some to commute to the capital and for others to find work locally. Some of the older, squalid property was swept away. Houses with their own indoor toilet and bath facilities were a great improvement on the difficult conditions endured by many in the first quarter of the 20th century. Hot water on tap may seem obvious today. But, 70 years ago residents in older properties had to boil large kettles and pans on open ranges. The bliss of clambering into a hot bath in privacy could not be underestimated. Although it felt some of the effects, Croydon did not suffer as badly from the depression years as they did in the industrial midlands and north country. By the time that the second world war began the town had become pleasantly residential. The middle classes were attracted to settle here, adding to Croydon's prosperity.

Right: It is almost like a scene from a Jimmy Cagney film as a chain gang wields picks and shovels. There was a large workforce employed on North End in 1926. It toiled away on the tramlines in front of Wilson's Tea Rooms. The workmen sweated away, most of them in the labourers' uniform of the day. Nearly everyone wore a cap, waistcoat, collarless shirt and sleeves rolled up to the elbow. The dress code was an unspoken form, but largely adhered to. The work was hard and backbreaking. Every stone, each clod of earth was dug out without the help of modern machinery. Wages were poor, but at least it was a job. In the 1920s unemployment was on the increase. The working class was not happy with its lot. This was the year of the General Strike. The work had attracted a large crowd of onlookers. Quite what is so fascinating about seeing men digging holes in the ground has never been explained. Perhaps it is just an excuse for those in suits to look down on someone carrying out manual work. Even young lads joined in the watching game. One of those on the left must have found it difficult to see everything going on. His fashionable cap obscured part of his vision. Compared with our fashions today, the youngster's headgear looks hilarious. Yet who can tell what our descendants will find a hoot about us 75 years from now?

The nurses at Queens were obviously a literary set. All of them in the sitting room at the nurses' home on Queens Road were engrossed in the newspapers and periodicals that gave them information about current affairs and showbiz gossip. These modern ladies of the lamp had largely worked within the National Health Service. One of their number, though, had been a carer before the welfare state was introduced. Her seniority is obvious from the form of head covering she wore as part of her formal uniform. This nurse, seated second right, had greater experience. It appears that she had seen active service during the war. She wore her

service ribbons on her tunic with pride. It was a less exciting time in which she now lived and worked. But, the work of the angels of mercy was no less important. It is just a pity that successive governments thought so little of their work and commitment that they were paid peanuts. The sitting room at the nurses' home was typical of the fashion of the early 1960s. Everything seemed to be box shaped. The fireplace and furniture were built with austere and regulation lines. Even whole houses conformed to that shape. Remember the folk singer, Pete Seegar, poking fun at the conformity of it all? He sang of 'Little boxes made of ticky tacky, and they all look just the same'.

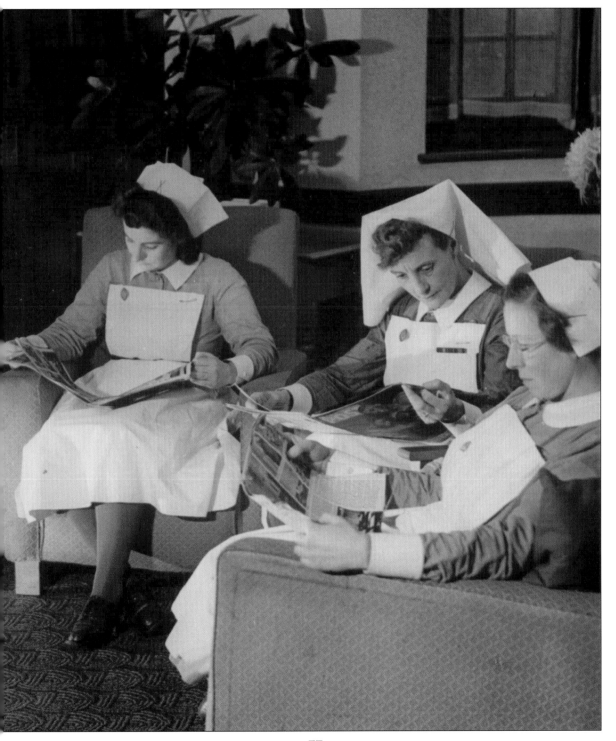

Above: Health and safety would have a field day with this scene today. Piles of reinforcing rods and metal spars litter the site. The scaffolding is only partly screened off. It would be so simple for someone to wander underneath the structure. A dropped spanner could cause a nasty injury. Up aloft there is not a hard hat in sight. The British workman regarded his skull as being thick enough without such namby pamby protection. It was 21 April 1948, after all. Had he not withstood bombs and bullets during the war? The dangers on a building site hardly compared with what he had been through. The building of Croydon 'B' Power Station was one of the first major postwar building works to be carried out. There had been a gas works on Surrey Street that was opened by the brewer Henry Overton in 1829. It was taken over by the Croydon Commercial Gas and Coke Company, building a new works at Waddon in 1866. Electricity was not introduced as a power source until later in the century. Many were frightened that it was dangerous. Despite those fears Croydon gained parliamentary approval for the introduction of electric light in 1891. The electric works opened on Factory Lane in 1896. It had an original capacity of 450 kilowatts. Service was provided to just 70 customers. This number rose to 793 by 1900. The new power station on Purley Way had been needed for some time because of increased demand. But for the war, work would have begun sooner.

Below: During the 19th century man harnessed coal and steam for much of his power. Great machines turned the wheels of the industrial revolution. In the next century electricity and oil added their influence. Turbines, pylons, mechanical diggers, cranes and the motor car changed our lives. They are all here somewhere in this March 1952 photograph. Yet, the most important resource can only just be seen heading towards the power station gates. It is manpower. He might be a mere speck in the distance, but without him none of this would operate. Pushing a humble wheelbarrow he might seem out of place amongst all the mechanised and automated technology around him. But who has to switch it all on? Who is to maintain and operate the plant? Who was it who thought it all up? Even the most sophisticated of equipment relies upon someone's control. The workman with his barrow probably had no time to consider his own importance. He just had a job to do. There was another pile of rubble to move, trench to dig or pipe to lay. He left such higher thoughts to others. There was enough to be done working on the temporary gable to the turbine and boiler house at the northerly end of Croydon 'B' Power Station. Not only that, but he had to think of something else for his sandwiches. The cheese ration had just been cut to an ounce a week.

Centre: The artist's impression of the new Barclays Bank shows it dominating the corner of Crown Hill, running down to the left. The main frontage of the building gives out onto North End. The artist deliberately exaggerated the power of the building, but it does stand out on this site, opposite the old Whitgift hospital and almshouses. Banking developed gradually from its first days. Early banks only verified coinage or exchanged one jurisdiction's coins for another's. As trade routes extended in the early Renaissance, bankers devised means for their agents to make payments at a distance. These were the forerunners of drafts and cheques. The first banks also accepted deposits of money or valuables for safekeeping. By the 17th century, London bankers had developed a system with most of the essentials of modern banking. They dealt in foreign exchange and paid interest to attract coin deposits. Central banks eventually replaced commercial banks as issuers of notes and currency. Barclays began banking about 300 years ago and now employs 57,000 in the UK. Over the last generation there has been a great shift in emphasis and style. Personal contact between customers and bank staff has decreased. We are just as likely to use the hole in the wall outside the bank as to enter the premises. Money can be moved by telephone and computer. We have pieces of plastic instead of cash. One day this building will be knocked down and replaced by a giant microchip.

Bottom: It is hard to know whether this is a bomb site or the start of something big. There is something almost unreal about the scene. Charlton Heston saw something similar when he returned to New York at the end of the film 'Planet of the Apes'. A nuclear holocaust had reduced many of the city's skyscrapers to rubble. Perhaps Croydon's developers inspired the movie. The timing was right. This was 5 March 1968, the year the Hollywood blockbuster came out. The office blocks dominated the skyline, just as they do now. Work was in progress on the flyover, as we look east towards the town centre from Duppas Hill. The flyover lifts traffic above High Street and on to the junction with Park Lane. Some of the concrete stanchions and pillars were already in place, but there were many months of work ahead before it could open to traffic. Croydon has been referred to as a mini Manhattan. You can see why from these towering offices. Since 1956 Croydon's central area adjoining the main suburban railway stations has been transformed by the development of multi storey buildings. Rising up with them have been the large shopping precinct and a cultural centre that includes the technical college, concert hall, and theatre. This area comprises England's largest concentration of office space outside central London. You can debate their architectural merits, but you cannot deny their existence. Like them or not, they are the heritage we are passing on to our children.

Right: The concrete piles, scaffolding and girders were a blight on the town in the 1960s. You cannot make an omelette without breaking eggs. Some disruption was necessary in the creation of Croydon's new face. As we lived through those times it did seem as if the building work would go on forever. This part of Park Lane was being altered to take the underpass. St George's House was under construction at the same time. Seen from the roof of the Fairfield Halls, the underpass would eventually carry traffic north and south under George Street. St George's House took over three years to complete. It was ready for occupation in 1965. Its 24 storeys dominated the old town. Charles Ellis erected the building to a design by Ronald Ward. The 260 feet high block was the town's tallest until 1970. St George's House was situated where the Greyhound Hotel once stood. The Greyhound had been one of the town's foremost coaching inns in better times. A place for the pub was found at the foot of the development, but it struggled to find a new identity. Various attempts to give it a new character were tried with limited success. In 1989 it was turned into the Blue Orchid night club. St George's House is now known as the Nestlé Building. The bird's nest logo of the company appeared on the tower block in 1994.

Below: Building work in the 1960s was everywhere. Look up or down and something was happening. New office blocks started to appear, stretching up into the clouds. There was also activity down below. The struts, girders and concrete are part of sections V to VIII of the underpass. Today cars appear from under the ground, like rabbits popping out of their holes. The photograph was taken from outside Electric House. It was surprisingly built in 1939-42 when most of the country's building programme ground to a halt. Norfolk House, on the other side of the underpass, was built in 1958-59. It was one of the first new developments to appear after the passing of the 1956 Croydon Corporation Act. Other notable structures along this section of Wellesley Road and Park Lane include Croydon College and Fairfield Halls. Robert Atkinson drew the original design for the college in the early 1950s. After his death his partner, Anderson, amended it. An extension was added in 1971. Fairfield Halls should have been built on the old railway sidings as a civic centre by the early 1940s. The war delayed the project. It was not until the early 1960s that it was revived. Croydon desperately needed a new entertainment centre. The late 1950s had kissed goodbye to the Public Halls, the Grand Theatre and the Davis Theatre. Fairfield Halls may not be the prettiest building, but it has given 40 years of good service for activities as diverse as wrestling and classical music.

A measured triumph

At the beginning of the 21st century it is difficult to imagine a world without electricity. Just as the stone age gave way to the bronze age, so the steam age has given way to the present electronic age. That transition began before any of us can now remember with only the very oldest, or those from remote rural areas, being able to recall life without electric lighting. But even the relatively young can recall life before video recorders, can recall their mother's first washing machine or perhaps seeing their first colour TV - or maybe even the first black and white television.

Certainly most readers of this book will remember the first time they saw a computer in real life as opposed to one in a science fiction film.

The electronic age did not happen overnight. The discoveries and inventions of famous scientists like Michael Faraday, Joseph Swann and Thomas Edison made them household names. But in truth the remorseless progress from the age of steam has depended just as much if not more on the cumulative work of thousands of unsung heroes each contributing in some small yet incremental part to the advancement of human knowledge. And Croydon can lay claim to a number of such entrepreneurs.

Above right: *The firm's original premises.* ***Left:*** *The interior of the firm's original premises.* ***Below:*** *At work in the 1960s.*

The Croydon Precision Instrument Company came into being on the 1st July 1952. The aim of the business was then, as it remains, to manufacture high quality electrical measuring instruments and standards. On 1st January 1977 the firm became a limited company and adopted the name by which it is now known: Cropico Ltd.

Back in 1952 four men had got together to found the new business: Warren Potter, Fred Dye, PA Bovey and FC Widdis. Warren Potter would concentrate on sales and administration whilst Fred Dye would apply his talent to the design and manufacture of the firm's products. Warren Potter eventually became company Chairman: today his son Michael Potter is Managing Director, the second generation of the family to work for the firm.

The fledgling firm at first occupied premises in Windmill Road where it would remain for the next few years. In 1957, five years after being founded, the company moved to its present location in Hampton Road.

Exactly like today copper, brass, aluminium, resistance alloys and precious metals would enter the premises to be turned into precision measuring instruments such as those used to test electrical voltage and resistance.

Since the company's manufacturing base has always been situated in Croydon many of the firm's highly experienced employees have been with the business since the 1950s giving not only continuity and stability but also ultimately helping to create the unique Cropico culture.

The company recognised that continuing success depends upon the introduction of new instruments and to that end Cropico quickly established an on-going programme of product development utilising new technology to the company's and customers' best advantage as it became available. Indeed the greatest challenge presented to the firm over the years since its foundation was the change from the design and manufacture of electromechanical instruments to modern digital equipment, including software. Cropico would eventually become one of the first companies in the world to manufacture and promote the use of solid state voltage standards.

The quality of the products stems from the design facilities at Cropico headed by the chief engineer Robert Coggan. Robert who joined the Cropico team in 1991 has a proven track record in the design of precision measuring standards and instruments.

Above: Some of the early precision measuring instruments made by Cropico.
Right: Cropico's products on display at an exhibition in Bilbao, Spain 1973.

Cropico has consistently focused its efforts on the challenge of maintaining its position at the forefront of the trade. Product development and innovation is viewed as essential to the company's continuing success, it therefore concentrates on the development of new products and ideas. The company believes that not only should its range of instruments give the best possible measurement results but also offer the customer confidence and reliability of measurement combined with low cost of ownership. The company's latest designs incorporate many advanced features such as multi-processor controls and a high level of digital integration combined with software-enhanced functionality which offers superb value for money.

Main markets today are manufacturers of electric motors and generators, transformers, cables, communication equipment manufacturers, defence equipment manufacturers, the aircraft industry, railways, the MOD, standards laboratories and test houses.

Despite hot competition from within Britain, as well as France and the USA, Cropico is thriving supplying instruments to a wide variety of customers, both large and small, including railways, the oil and gas industry, electricity generation and distribution, cable manufacturers, the pharmaceutical industry and universities.

The use of Croprico low thermal 'emf' switches on the Russian oil pipeline requires them to withstand temperatures of -40 degrees; in the USA NASA uses the company's precision thermometers. A contract has also been won to supply Canadian Pacific Railways with the firm's ohmmeters for the

measurement of signalling circuits. The absence of any failure in the original instrument supplied led the Canadian Pacific Railways CN Signal and Communication Division to purchase a further 50 of Cropico's highly sophisticated portable digital milliohmmeters for use across its countrywide rail signal system; the instruments are used to determine cable resistance and measure bonding, battery-to-rail and relay-to-rail resistance values on the 20V DC rail signal system where temperatures can fall to -10c or less.

The latest developments by the company have improved the design of previous products adding new measurements to models and making the Cropico range one of the most exciting and technically advanced on the market. An example of the most recent developments is the series 3000 thermometers, an impressive range of precision digital thermometers; all models are accurate to 0.01 degrees Celsius and have a resolution of 0.001 degrees with other options and features to suit most applications and budgets.

Whilst few of us will encounter Cropico's products in our daily lives nevertheless each of us will have indirectly benefited from its work. Electricity is anonymous; we consume it everywhere giving little thought to where it comes from and what technologies may need to be applied to make it safe and effective. It is companies like Cropico that over the last fifty years or more have helped the electronics age arrive, ensuring that invisibly, behind the scenes, our lives can continue to be enriched by the marvels of modern technology.

Top left: *Cropico's staff in 1996.*
Above: *One of Cropico's latest products.*
Below: *Warren Potter, Chairman and Michael Potter, MD receiving the ISO 9000 certificate, 1996.*

Cementing the past

Cement. Where would we be without that building material? Without its invention we might still be living in wattle and daub houses rather than the brick, stone and concrete edifices we live in today. At first sight Croydon might not be thought of as the cement capital of Britain - it has no cement works - and yet the town is well known to the cement industry through the firm of FL Smidth Ltd.

FL Smidth is the UK subsidiary of the Danish multi-national business FLS Industries.

The firm designs, builds and services cement production factories world-wide with more than 50 per cent of current world cement production through FLS process plants.

FLS was founded in Denmark in 1882 by Frederik Lassoe Smidth and two partners, Messrs. Larsen and Foss, who built their first cement works at Limhamm in Sweden in 1888. The firm had been formed initially to construct brickworks and flour mills but turned its attention to the manufacture of cement with remarkable success. A London office was opened in 1890 in a single room in Bridge Street, Westminster to handle the growing global market for cement, particularly in English speaking countries.

The company had various offices in and around London until 1966 when it, and its then subsidiary Tunnel Cement, acquired the ten-story building at 17, Lansdowne Road, Croydon which it has occupied ever since.

In 1966 Croydon was being developed to relieve central London and was an ideal location not simply for access to the capital but also for Gatwick airport.

Although there are no cement producers in Croydon (in fact there are only four producers in the whole UK) FLS has good relationships with many local engineering companies and suppliers.

Fortunately for the local engineering companies and FLS there is no substitute for cement on the horizon and FLS expects to remain in business for many years to come, and remain in Lansdowne Road for the foreseeable future. That commitment is underpinned by continuity: the third generation descendants of Frederik Smidth's partners are still involved with the company founded so long ago in Denmark.

Above left: Mr Frederik Lassoe Smidth, who founded the company in 1882. Below left: Modern cement plant in Asia. Below: The firm's British Headqarters on Lansdowne Road, Croydon.

Whitgift Hospital - the other Whitgift legacy

The Foundation Stones of the Hospital of the Holy Trinity at Croydon were laid by John Whitgift, Archbishop of Canterbury in 1596. It was operational three years later, having been established for the maintenance of between thirty and forty 'poor, needy or impotent people' from the parishes of Croydon and Lambeth, who received, as well as their lodging, a small regular stipend. The grammar school was attached to the hospital at this time and the two branches of the foundation existed side by side until the mid 1800s when the educational side started to develop the much higher profile it has today.

The hospital buildings are two-storeyed and surround an interior quadrangle measuring about 76 by 82 ft. The materials are red brick, with occasional black brick and flint and stucco dressings and on the three gables the letters J W, J C and J W in blue brick indicate alternately John Whitgift and Joannes Cantuarensis (John, Archbishop of Canterbury).

The hospital buildings came under numerous threats of demolition on account of Croydon Corporation's road-widening plans. However the Whitgift Hospital was saved by the intervention of the House of Lords. It is now a scheduled building under the terms of the Town and Country Planning Acts.

In 1969 Parliament passed the Whitgift Charity Act which widened the powers of the Whitgift Foundation's Governors, especially in relation to the Hospital. Two years later, in 1971 the Foundation was granted its own armorial bearings by the College of Arms.

A programme of extensive restoration was undertaken and a plaque commemorating this work was unveiled by Her Majesty Queen Elizabeth II when she paid a visit to the Hospital on June 21 1983. She signed the Visitors' Book and was shown, amongst other items, Queen Elizabeth I's seal on the Founder's Letters Patent to found a Hospital, dated 22 November 1595.

The foundation stone of Whitgift House at Haling Park, providing sheltered accommodation and residential care for some 40 elderly people, was laid by Archbishop Runcie, Visitor to the Foundation, in 1984. He returned four years later to perform the opening ceremony when the building was furnished and equipped for use.

Above left: *John Whitgift.*
Right: *The entrance to Whitgift Hospital.*
Below: *A bird's eye view of the Quadrangle at Whitgift Hospital.*

Whitgift School - four centuries of development

Now entering its fifth century, Whitgift School is highly esteemed among the schools of Britain. It is a major independent boys' day school with a strong academic profile. The environment is a stimulating one within which every boy has the opportunity, in the pursuit of excellence, to develop his potential to the full.

The school occupies a beautiful 45-acre parkland site and has almost incomparable facilities, with a record of outstanding achievement in academic work, music, games and extra-curricular activities.

Many scholarships and bursaries, including some free places, are available so that parents of prospective pupils may apply regardless of their income. Whitgift is easily accessible, and boys come from widely different backgrounds and feeder schools in London, Surrey, Kent and Sussex.

The School was founded in 1596 as a grammar school (ie for the teaching of Latin and Greek) by John Whitgift, Elizabeth I's last Archbishop of Canterbury, and opened in the centre of Croydon in 1600. The present Headmaster, Dr Christopher Barnett, is the twenty-sixth in the school's history.

During the first hundred and fifty years of its existence it was distinguished for the quality of its teaching of the classics, the staple for entry to the Universities and the Inns of Court and for the instruction of the professional and other educated classes. Pupils attended not only as local day-boys but also as boarders from the home counties and even further afield. There was special provision for free education "of the poorer sort" of the parish of Croydon. Among the early pupils were several who came to occupy positions of importance in the State, including Baron Percy of Alnwick, Governor of Jersey 1640; the Earl of Carbery, Lord Lieutenant of the Marches 1660; Sir Daniel Harvey, Ambassador to Constantinople 1660; Scroop Egerton, first Duke of Bridgewater 1720.

Above right: *Whitgift School's original buildings of 1600.*
Right: *Whitgift School viewed from the rear in the 1880s.*

By 1800, however, the curriculum imposed by the Founder's Statutes was not to the taste of generations that required a more practical education for their sons, with the result that numbers declined - in common with many other ancient grammar schools - and at times during the nineteenth century the Schoolmaster took no pupils at all.

In 1871 the School was reactivated through a scheme of the Court of Chancery and provided with new premises in North End close to the old Elizabethan buildings, which were demolished less than 30 years later. The School gained a fresh reputation, and in 1907 its Headmaster, S O Andrew, was elected a member of the Headmasters' Conference. Among the men of distinction who were at school in North End were many academics and professional men; Sir James Berry, President of the Royal Society of Medicine 1926; two Chiefs of the Air Staff: Major General Sir Frederick Sykes and Marshal of

It is closely associated with the London Mozart Players, who perform there and give master classes; in 2000 the Royal Albert Hall was taken over for a performance of Verdi's Requiem.

In sport the School's reputation stands high as winners of inter-school tournaments at various levels, rugby, cricket, hockey and most recently fencing (being Schools Champions for the last two years), all with many international representatives, indicating a truly eclectic range of achievement. Boys also have opportunities to involve themselves in local community service, charity work and fund raising. There are commitments to children with learning difficulties, to such projects as Riding for the Disabled and helping at the Whitgift Foundation's homes for the elderly.

The Old Whitgiftian Association has its own clubhouse and grounds nearby, where rugby, cricket and hockey are played, and where reunions and social events are held. Among the many Old Whitgiftians of fame who have attended the School at Haling Park have been Members of Parliament, innumerable university professors and other men of learning, bishops, diplomats, judges and Queen's Counsel, war heroes and service-men of distinction, including Group Captain John Cunningham, night-fighter pilot. Sportsmen have proliferated, including rugby internationals Martin Turner, Ian Beer (Headmaster of Harrow 1981) and Alan Wordsworth, and the test cricketer Raman Subba Row. Other notables are politicians Lords Prentice, Freeman, Bowness and Tope, and performance artists Guy Woolfenden, Martin Jarvis and Jeremy Sams. The current President of the OWA is Sir David Hancock, KCB.

the RAF Lord Tedder; civil servants, including Lord Trend; lawyers including Lord Diplock; diplomats including Sir Gordon Whitteridge; sportsmen including rugby internationals Peter Brook and Basil Nicholson.

In the 1920s it became clear that the North End site of about 10 acres and its buildings, although considerably augmented since 1871, were inadequate for the School's growth. The Governors purchased the remaining portion of historic Haling Park, South Croydon, the former home of Lord Howard of Effingham, Lord High Admiral of the Fleet sent against the Armada. The new buildings were opened by HRH Prince George in 1931.

These comprise a handsome quadrangle, a capacious assembly hall (Big School) and a range of structures that remain a dignified core well adapted for the changing requirements of modern times. They have been supplemented by many extensions of exceptional quality, including a music school, concert hall, sports-hall complex, indoor swimming pool, junior school building; in 1990 one of the largest and most innovative educational building projects in Britain was completed to provide integrated facilities for science, technology, art and design, together with a new library and resource centre.

Whitgift is justly proud of its varied musical life and has for many years hosted the Croydon Musical Festival, which brings many musicians to perform at the School.

The start of the new millennium saw the School visited by the Independent Schools Inspectorate: it received a commendation of the highest kind.

Top left: *Big School.* ***Above left:*** *The School in its parkland setting.* ***Below:*** *Her Majesty Queen Elizabeth II and the Junior School Orchestra, 16 February 1996.*

An enrichment of the best sort

Trinity School is now a major independent day school with outstanding facilities and a reputation for achievement in a very wide range of activities as well as high academic standards. It is a far cry from its traceable origins as a distinctive school in the 1850s though it does owe its foundation and its being to Archbishop John Whitgift, who established education as one of the two elements of his Foundation in Croydon. Trinity has always taken particularly to heart Whitgift's instruction to 'teach freely certain children of the parish of Croydon of the poorer sort' and had kept its doors as wide open as possible to boys of potential, whatever their parents' means.

By 1850, the educational side of Whitgift's Foundation had virtually withered away. The school room had since 1812 been let (without fee) to the National Society, who for 1d a week provided a very basic training in reading and writing and instruction in the Holy Scriptures. Croydon was growing rapidly with the arrival of the railways and the demand for a decent education led to civic pressure groups to energise those responsible for Whitgift's Foundation. As a result, a scheme with the first representative Governing Body was approved in 1856 to build two schools, a 'poor' school and a

Top Left: *The School's first Headmaster, William Ingrams.* ***Above right:*** *A cricket match at North End in the early 1960s.* ***Right:*** *The Whitgift Middle School Photographic Society pictured in 1898.* ***Below:*** *Staff pictured in 1910.*

'middle-class or commercial' school. Available funds meant that only one could be started and the Vicar of Croydon's dominance meant that it was the 'poor' school. It opened in 1858 on newly built premises in Church Road in the heart of the parish. William Ingrams, who had been appointed as Master of the National School in 1850 when 20, was appointed Head. A remarkable man, he remained Headmaster of the School and its successor until 1905 and was clearly a much respected and beloved figure.

The poor School was for boys aged 7 to 14 who lived in the parish of Croydon and who were 'able to read and not afflicted with any infectious or noisome disease' - 4d a week was the maximum to be charged. The Master was to take them to church

Whitgift Shopping Centre. A major challenge from the late 1970s was to maintain the level and quality of intake after the Direct Grant System was abolished. As the school flourished and became larger, so new buildings were approved until the present remarkable provision was achieved.With full use of the Government Assisted Places Scheme and subsequently the Foundation's own bursary scheme, Trinity has consciously set itself to remain true to the founder's intention, interpreted in modern terms to provide an excellent education for those boys who can benefit from it, whatever their parents' income.

every Sunday. The School was popular and successful. Inspection reports in the 1870s were glowing. However, the introduction of full provision for primary education led to the Poor School becoming an anachronism which the Charity Commission wished to abolish. After lengthy debate, it closed in December 1881, and Whitgift Middle School opened the following term in the same buildings. Mr Ingrams was appointed Head, and a number of pupils, whose parents could weather the financial leap to £2-5-0 a term, joined him.

Whitgift Middle School was designated a Third Grade Secondary School - the grade reflecting the specific purpose, not the quality! It was geared to provide a suitable education for those leaving at 14 or 15 to enter commercial occupations. It was a popular and successful school which gradually increased its aspirations. Great concern about the buildings in which it was housed led eventually to its removal to North End, which had been vacated by Whitgift School. This became its home from 1931-1965. To remove confusion, its name was changed in 1954 to 'Trinity School of John Whitgift'.

The Foundation had always been relatively well funded; its income was transformed in the 1960s. The Shirley Hotel was bought and Trinity moved to its present site in 1965, North End subsequently being developed as the

Top left: *Some of Trinity's musicians.* **Top right:** *HRH Prince Philip during a visit to the school in 1996.* **Above right:** *Sir Douglas Bader opening facilities for disabled pupils in 1981.* **Right:** *The modern streamlined school at the start of the 21st century.*

A legacy of care and excellence

Many people consider Croydon to be a recently-established centre, but the Old Palace School gives the lie to this mistaken impression. It was founded in 1889, when Victoria was Queen, by the Sisters of the Church, an Anglican religious community, who had at their head a remarkable woman called Emily Ayckbowm. She was very different from many women who founded girls' schools around that time in that, although she possessed a formidable brain, she was not an academic, nor was she a campaigner for women's rights - she didn't have to be, she got her own way by force of her own character. She stood out with determination against prejudice, ignorance, class consciousness and, when necessary, the 'Establishment'. The School has good reason to be proud of their Founder, she was a woman, cast in a rare mould, who deserves to take a very high place among the women of her day.

The School has a long tradition of social and charitable work which has responded to different needs as society's needs themselves have changed over the years.

The aim has always been to widen the horizons of girls' concerns beyond the immediate neighbourhood, to contribute to the awareness of suffering in different parts of the world and above all to give practical help. Mother Emily would certainly approve of this.

The School became a Direct Grant Grammar School in 1945. In 1974, with the ending of the Direct Grant, the Sisters withdrew from the School which then became an independent day School. In 1993 the School became a part of the Whitgift Foundation.

The Old Palace from which the School takes its name, was a former residence of the Archbishops of Canterbury and was presented to the Sisters of the Church in 1887 by the 7th Duke of Newcastle-under-Lyme, who, though still an undergraduate at Oxford, bought the Old Palace buildings to save them from demolition. They were at that time almost in ruins and

Above: *An old school photo from the early 1900s.*
Below: *A deputation of Old Palace pupils representing Scotland at a pageant at Lambeth Palace, circa 1912.*

Mother Emily was at first inclined to refuse it for religious use for which the Duke offered it. The Chapel, Great Hall and Library still form an integral part of the working facilities of the School. The historic buildings have been complemented by modern purpose-built ones and there is a continuing programme of new building and refurbishment in line with modern educational trends: for example, in 1993, the School opened a new Arts and Technology Annexe and in 1999 a new swimming pool. A new Preparatory School building will be completed in 2001, as will the new Sixth Form, Dining and PE facilities.

Old Palace School aims to provide a sound education based on Christian ideals. Students are encouraged to work hard and develop their potential so they may achieve satisfying careers. The need to equip girls to live in a rapidly changing world is fully appreciated so they can respond with confidence to developments in society, to environmental issues and technological advances.

From its inception the School has welcomed visits from past pupils who can inspire present pupils to go on and achieve similar greatness as their predecessors, and the School has a flourishing and active Old Girls' Society.

The School aims to provide a caring, stable and consistent setting in which girls can develop as individuals and where they know that in any difficulty they can be assured of help and understanding. High standards of courtesy and care are encouraged. In addition to a strong emphasis on core curriculum subjects there are good facilities for music, drama, art and technology and the essential experience of the latest information and communication technology. Excellent examination results have led to high ranking in the league tables.

The Old Palace Sixth Form provides opportunity for the transition from a highly structured learning environment to one in which girls take

responsibility for their own progress and development. Joint activities with other schools in the area are undertaken. The School's aim is that girls should leave the Sixth Form as well-qualified, confident and caring young women ready to make a useful contribution to the community.

The overall aim of the curriculum teaching and general ethos of the School is to give girls a wide and liberal education, a love of learning and scholarship and a pleasure in those things of spiritual and intellectual worth which will enable them to live a full life.

Top left: Her Majesty Queen Elizabeth during her visit to the school in November 1960. ***Above right:*** *HRH Prince Philip talking to Duke of Edinburgh Award winners at the school entrance on Old Palace Road, when he and Her Majesty the Queen visited the school in 1996.* ***Right:*** *Heritage Day at Old Palace School, October 2000.* ***Below:*** *The front of the School.*

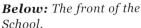

The art of education

Croydon College is prominently situated adjacent to the Fairfield Halls concert venue in the heart of Croydon town centre. The history of the College is directly linked to that of two institutions which, in effect, merged to form the present college in 1974. These were Croydon College of Art and Croydon Polytechnic.

Today Croydon College is one of the largest colleges of Further and Higher Education in the country with a student population of 13,000. The College offers a wide range of programmes from Foundation to Degree level and beyond; it is the sole provider of Higher Education within the Borough.

Around 75 per cent of students are studying for FE programmes and 25 per cent on HE programmes. In response to students' needs, programmes are offered in a variety of modes with 36 per cent of students attending full time and 64 per cent part time. Part time students either study during the day or evening, or via open/distance learning.

Croydon College is affiliated to the University of Sussex which provides many of the advantages associated with that of a highly regarded university.

The College also benefits from a dedicated Higher Education Centre and a state-of-the-art library and learning support facility.

Croydon is justifiably proud of its College which, back in 1988, celebrated its centenary. It was in 1888 that a worried government urged local authorities to increase technical education to help the country keep pace with our industrial competitors in Europe - particularly Germany - with the slogan 'Intelligent youths of the artisan class should have access to technical schools'.

In response Croydon founded its own technical institute. The Pitlake Technical Institute (which would later become the Croydon Polytechnic) was founded by the Reverend Oakley Coles the curate at the Parish Church with an initial intake of just 162 students.

Courses were designed and assessed for a wide variety of crafts by organisations such as City and Guilds. Theory was taught by 'talk and chalk' followed by practical sessions in the workshops which enabled apprentices

Above: *An example of an early prospectus.*
Below: *An artist's impression of the new Croydon College in November 1959.*

Local Education Authority. The first new block was opened in Scarbrook Road on 22nd December 1891 by the Archbishop of Canterbury Dr EW Benson; Reverend Coles was appointed the Polytechnic's Honorary Director.

In 1892 branches of the Croydon Polytechnic opened in South Norwood and Thornton Heath due to ever-increasing demand for places - followed in 1897 with a short-lived branch at Purley.

Meanwhile the Art School had received its first public funds with a grant from Croydon Council made in 1895.

A large extension was made to the Polytechnic building in Scarbrook Road in 1902 and the following year the running of the polytechnic was taken over by the newly formed Croydon Education Committee.

to progress up a numbered ladder of paper qualifications on a served time basis. The room where instruction first took place still exists with windows sufficiently high to avoid distraction and the legend 'Croydon Polytechnic' tells that through these doors entered the embryo engineers, printers, carpenters and draughtsmen who would save the country from the threat of Europe.

In fact the Croydon College story goes back rather further than 1888. Twenty years earlier in 1868 the School (later the College) of Art had been founded above the Public Halls in George Street. It would however take many more decades for the two Colleges' destinies to coincide.

In 1890 however the Council voted £3,000 to fund the creation of a Polytechnic; it set up a Polytechnic Committee to move things forward even though this was a full 12 years before the establishment of the

The Edwardian era and the years of the Great War of 1914-18 were periods of first consolidation followed by a shift of the national focus away from education to the war effort and to subsequent economic depression. Further development would have to wait another decade.

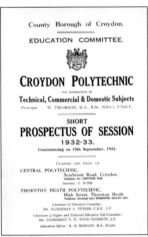

Top left: The College begining to take shape in 1956. Above left: The College under construction in the early 1950s. Above right: The frontispiece of a prospectus from 1932. Right: First students at the new Technical College, 28th September 1955.

It was in 1929 that the Board of Education first urged the need for a new technical college to replace the Croydon Polytechnic - although it would still be many years before action could be taken.

In 1932 the School of Art however was taken over by the Council to become Croydon College of Art. Meanwhile at the Polytechnic, the mid 1930s would see the first ever day classes where evening classes had only existed before.

Plans for the new technical college finally were drawn up by 1939 but the advent of yet another war inevitably halted any further progress.

Top: A fine exhibition of work by art students, 1930. **Above:** *A lecture taking place on the 28th September 1955.* **Right:** *An aerial view of the college in October 1964.*

And worse was to follow: in 1941 the Polytechnic was gutted by fire. Nor was that the only fire, in 1947 seven firemen were injured when flames swept the George Street premises of the Croydon School of Art causing extensive damage and gutting part of that building too. The fire had started in the general office and soon spread to a number of other rooms; arriving firemen found the second floor of the office block and the roof well alight before the fire could be brought under control.

It was to be 1948 before the plans for a new college could be revived when the Council drew up a Development Plan for Further Education. By then student enrolment had risen to over 4,000. The plan was to create a technical college which would bring the Polytechnic and College of Art under one roof.

Three years later the Council formally approved plans for a new college and in 1953 building work could

Venus as the image to represent their work and to precede them into the new premises.

More building would soon follow: by 1963 plans were in hand for a new 12 storey tower block at the Fairfield site to provide additional accommodation for Croydon's College of Art. Building was however deferred and, no doubt to students' disappointment, a swimming pool was omitted from the fourth building stage in order to reduce costs.

It was not until 1969 that building could eventually begin on the £500,000 tower block to house the College of Art which would move some departments there in 1971 after completion of the first phase of building work.

start at the Fairfield site on the first of four stages. Lord Tedder would lay the foundation stone in 1954 whilst the building was dedicated by Geoffrey Fisher, then Archbishop of Canterbury.

The new building would occupy a site of almost four acres and eventually cost £1.5 million. The site would incorporate the Denning Hall, a bequest for the advancement of education in the town made by Mrs Elizabeth Denning the widow of a former Mayor (1913-16) and sited in the courtyard between the two east wings

Despite a disastrous flood on the site that year, on 28th September 1955, the new principal, Hugh Falkner opened the doors of Croydon Technical College for the first time.

Building work however continued. It would be another five years before the official opening ceremony would take place when in November 1960 the Queen visited Croydon to do the honours, a plaque in the College foyer commemorates the occasion.

The Queen was not the only dignitary to attend that year. In June, Venus the Goddess of Love had made her way down George Street standing in a miniature racing car. She was wearing goggles and a crash helmet and preceded by heralds who cleared the way before her and the mourners which followed her. The occasion, staged by students, was part of the ceremony put on by Croydon Art School which moved from premises in Coombe Road to the new Technical College. The students had decided to use

The formal merger of the two colleges occurred in 1974. On 1st September 1974, the year the second phase of the new College of Art was completed, both the College of Art and the Technical College came under one body as Croydon College of Design and Technology, though still with separate prospectuses. It was not to be until 1978 that Croydon College of Design and Technology would acquire its present name of Croydon College.

In 1984 the Heath Clark Tertiary Centre was opened and in 1987 the Selhurst Tertiary Centre also became part of the College.

Now, at the beginning of the 21st Century, Croydon College still meets the aims and objectives of its founders: a sound technical and artistic education to provide the community with the skills they, and employers need, to face the future with confidence.

Top left: *Students in the School of Art.* ***Right:*** *A view of the college in May 1997.*

Sparks of genius

According to one of England's greatest scientists Lord Kelvin 'When you can measure what you are talking about and express it in numbers you know something about it'. Lord Kelvin's summing up of the value of a system of electrical measurement in 1861 led directly to five units of electrical measurement being named after the most famous names in the field: M. Ampere, GS Ohm, Volta, Joseph Henry and Michael Faraday.

Thirty years later a young man bored with his job wrote on his diary that he had 'said goodbye once and for all to clerical work' and began a new career. This was the origin of the well known Tinsley electronic instrument company

The company was founded by Henry Tinsley in 1904. At the age of 19 Tinsley had already been working for

Above: Company founder, Henry Tinsley.
Right: Working conditions in 1919.
Below: Becoming more labour intensive, 1925.

eight years as an errand boy earning two shillings (10p) per week and a little later had taken a job as a clerk at five shillings per week working for a wool broker. He first became interested in technical matters whilst browsing in the Guildhall library which prompted him to make his crucial career change. He went on to work for a number of scientific instrument manufacturing companies the first of which was Muirheads & Co, for whom he worked first as a labourer before working his way up the firm to occupy evermore demanding positions. No matter how hard or menial the task Tinsley always kept his eyes and ears open at Muirheads and in addition used his leisure wisely by joining the electrical classes run by the Goldsmiths' Technical College. After obtaining a certificate from there he

was put on the staff at Muirheads and within a short time was helping with the drawings and designs. Altogether Tinsley spent some nine years with

Muirheads and obtained a wide knowledge of the growing electrical industry until he left to work for Cambridge Instruments and later RW Paul & Co. for a short time before founding his own business.

Tinsley would go on to pioneer the design and manufacture of a range of electrical measuring instruments including those for temperature, voltage and resistance measuring as well as capacitors and detectors used in submarine cable work. Over the following century some thousands of different instruments would be designed by his firm, some selling in large numbers others as unique items designed for a single purpose for a single customer.

In the year that he founded his own firm Henry Tinsley was living in a house called 'Pen Lea' in Elmers Road, Beckenham and started the business from a small workshop at his home where he took on his first employee, William Moat.

Equipped with little more than a single lathe Tinsley began making resistance boxes and galvanometers. The business quickly grew and in 1907 the firm moved to Stanley House, Eldon Park Road, South Norwood when Tinsley entered into a partnership with another instrument maker named Snell becoming for a short time Snell & Tinsley making telegraph apparatus, condensers, standard cells, potentiometers and 'bridges'. Snell however was destined to die after one year of the partnership leaving Henry Tinsley in sole ownership - though with financial

Top: Staff pictured in 1936.
Above: Working conditions in 1936.
Right: An advertisement for Tinsley's Galvonometers, 1919.

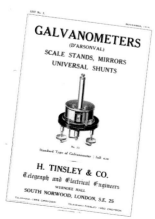

difficulties which would only be overcome by taking almost nothing out of the business for some time.

Fortunately during those difficult early years Henry Tinsley would be assisted by his wife Emma a frugal Quaker who kept a very close eye on the finances and also helped in many practical tasks, cell making and coil winding. She was considerably older than her husband and claimed to be one of the first female typists in England having been trained by the Remington Company to demonstrate their products.

At the time of the firm's formation scientific instrument making was still in its infancy and products were being continually updated almost from

batch to batch as the technology progressed and new materials were introduced. Instrument making was a very labour intensive business in those days with virtually everything contained within the instruments being made on the premises, including the very fine teak cases which were then were synonymous with precision instruments.

When Henry Tinsley started the company he worked very closely with the National Physical Laboratory at Teddington which had been founded just a few years earlier. 'Tinsley's' have been manufacturing instruments based on NPL designs ever since

The firm's next base, Werndee Hall, South Norwood, had been built in 1883 and was originally owned by the Smith family; it later became a school for young gentlemen but for a while had been left empty. With the business

Top left: An advertisement for a Potentiometer, 1929. **Right:** *Mr and Mrs Tinsley.* **Far right:** *Werndee Hall, South Norwood.* **Below:** *A staff gathering, 1964, with a total combined service of over 600 years.*

company in 1919 to become Scientific Director of the Admiralty Experimental Station.

Shortly after the end of the first world war, following CV Drysdale's departure, Henry Tinsley was joined by a young cousin, DC Gall. Upon Tinsley's retirement in 1934 DC Gall would eventually become sole owner and Chief Executive of the business which he would run up until 1970 - by which time he was being assisted by his two sons Maurice and Colin Gall.

DC Gall joined the firm in 1919 on his release from the Royal Navy Air Service. With a view to becoming an eventual partner the young man was put in charge of the test room and under his more practical grasp manufacturing efficiency was soon improved and piled up orders from home and abroad were soon sorted out and systematically executed. Among the many developments which followed Gall's appointment was a considerable diversification of production. This meant finding the instrumentation needs of as wide a range of industries and branches

now rapidly expanding Tinsley was looking for new premises and moved into Werndee Hall in 1916 where the firm would stay for almost 70 years.

Werndee Hall consisted of a large house and stable, the building was on a three acre site which was ideally suited to handling the expansion of the business which had occurred due to the war when many new and varied instruments were required by the military.

For a brief period Tinsley was joined by a partner, Dr CV Drysdale, who was an eminent scientist, head of Electrical and Applied Physics at Northampton Institute, an Examiner to the Spectacle Makers Company and President of the Optical Society as well as a Fellow of the Royal Statistical Society and, controversially at the time, President of the Malthusian League devoted to promoting the then taboo subject of birth control. Drysdale left the

Top left and right: *Staff pictured in 1963.*
Above left: *Stanley House, Eldon Park Road, South Norwood.* ***Below:*** *Mr D C Gall, centre, Mr Maurice Gall, left, Mr Colin Gall, right.*

of physics as possible, so that when orders fell off in one direction there would be other possible markets. That steady diversification increased the number of types of instrument produced and compensated for fluctuating demand. Over the decades which followed a considerable number of instruments made by Tinsley would bear some mark of D C Gall's influence, many of them had been designed by him and in the process acquiring more than 50 patents in his name

Long before then however, still in the early days of the firm, some very strange techniques were used for manufacturing: one of those was the winding of special electrical coils - the written instructions for manufacture attached to the drawing required the operator to tie one end of the wire to a tree in the garden at Werndee Hall and then walk down the garden winding the wire on a bobbin.

Both pictures: *Work becomes more technical in the late 1960s.*

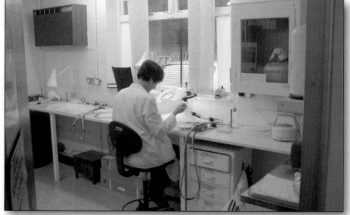

Both the first and second world wars would have a marked and profound effect on the Tinsley business; the demand for instruments greatly increased, many employees left to join the services - some never to return. During the first world war amongst instruments made purely for the war effort were aeroplane compasses, inclinometers and mine detecting devices an increase in demand which would be repeated in 1939. During the second world war apart from some minor blast damage Werndee Hall miraculously escaped the attention of enemy bombers despite being an obvious target with its two prominent towers and production actually increase tenfold from pre-war levels.

Over the years the business has built up an enviable reputation for the design and manufacture of electrical measuring instruments and is regarded as one of the leading companies in its field. Its customer base is wide and includes virtually all sections of manufacturing and engineering as well as Standards Laboratories both national and within particular industries both at home and abroad.

The firm began exporting its products overseas almost from its inception. That position remains to the present time with over 40 agents representing Tinsley throughout the world as well as having its own offices in the USA and India. Exports make up 70 per cent of sales with the largest orders in the company's history coming from the People's Republic of China during the 1950s and 60s with orders for hundreds of different types of instruments being placed and shipped to China - even on one

occasion being sent aboard a Chinese trawler fleet which called at Hull when other docks were closed due to a industrial dispute.

For its first 50 years, unlike the present day, 'Tinsley's' did not employ sales engineers apart from the occasions when Henry Tinsley himself or his nephew visited customers to discuss their requirements - the company simply relied on its reputation to sell its products. It was not until the early 1950s that the firm would employ its first full time technical sales representative; thereafter sales engineers would travel throughout the UK and abroad visiting the company's agents, arranging exhibitions of the firm's products and spreading the company's reputation still further.

And what a reputation! In the late 1960s one of the firm's representatives visited the original Ferranti factory in Oldham near Manchester where Ferranti manufactured Watt-hour meters used in household electric meters. The visit was made to inspect a quantity of Tinsley watt-meters being used on the production line with the idea of refurbishing them. Many of the instruments were over fifty years old and had been in continuous use the whole time. Fifteen of the instruments were indeed returned to the Tinsley factory and refurbished and were still in use at the end of the 20th century at what is now Siemens Metering Instruments. A watt-meter of this type was at one time even exhibited at the Science Museum and another is at the NPL museum in Teddington.

Yet another story of Tinsley's legendary reliability came in 1986 when Professor BR Coles the Dean of the Royal College of Science at Imperial College sent

a photograph of a Diesselhorst Potentiometer bought by the Physics Department of Imperial College in 1924 and still in use.

Over the years many hundreds, even thousands, of local people have worked for Tinsley. Hundreds of apprentices have passed through the company, many going on to hold senior positions, and in some cases

Above left: *Galvanometer Department.* ***Left:*** *Specialist coil winding.*

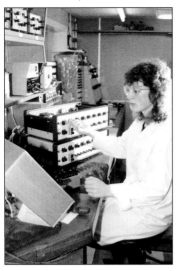

directorships, in companies of well known engineering business. All will have fond memories of their time with Tinsley which in many ways was like working in one big family, something which the firm still tries to foster to this day.

How many of those ex-apprentices now recall their days at 'Tinsley's' one wonders? When new apprentices were assisting the senior staff in the workshop they were often sent to the stores to get ridiculous things as a joke; one such item was a 'skirting board ladder'. The store keeper had been called on so many times for this non-existent item that he eventually had a miniature ladder made around eight inches long and issued it to the surprised youngsters and let them turn the joke back on the senior men.

Not that apprentices couldn't look after themselves. The youngest apprentices were expected to make tea for everyone and one man in the test room was very particular about where his cup had to be placed, throwing a tantrum if his tea was placed in the wrong spot. One day an apprentice took his revenge by drilling a hole in the bottom of the cup and screwing it to the man's bench then filling it with tea. The bad tempered older man in a fury at seeing his tea in the wrong spot went to knock it to the floor and instead merely succeeded in breaking the bottom from the cup and spilling tea over himself, he didn't complain again.

A capacity for fun seems to have survived the decades. Ever more stringent methods of measuring and controlling humidity have been used over the years to ensure the quality of the firm's production techniques; the humidity is tested by

external auditors: Each year the humidity measuring instruments demanded by the auditors became more sophisticated moving from early instruments which used the contraction and expansion of a human hair, through to wet and dry thermometers and most recently on to electronic sampling instrumentation. Anticipating the auditors next visit and their demand for even more complex measuring devices staff constructed the ultimate hi-tech instrument - at the core of which was a fir cone which opened in the wet and closed in the dry!

A light hearted approach could however sometimes backfire. When an extension was being built to the test room which would require builders to remove a brick from the wall to let in a steel girder staff ran a sweep on which brick would be removed; each member of staff put a cross on the brick they had chosen and signed it. Unfortunately a confused work man seeing the crosses thought they were instructions to take out all the marked bricks and it would be many weeks before the large whole was filled, leaving the unhappy gamblers to suffer the discomfort of draughts and breezes.

Despite building extensions, in 1983, given the considerable amount of work which would be required to bring the building up to a modern standard Werndee Hall and the surrounding land were sold and the company moved to Imperial Way on the Old Croydon Airport Estate. And in 1991 the company moved again to its current premises, a 25,000 sq. ft factory in King Henry's Drive, New Addington.

The business has never been afraid to change. As a small company employing approximately 50 people

Above left: *Calibration Laboratory.*
Below: *The company's premises at Imperial Way on the Old Croydon Airport Estate.*

instruments manufactured today are of an accuracy which was unheard of when Henry Tinsley founded the business but one can be sure he would have been proud of the progress that has been made in the half century since his death in 1950 aged 78. His company continues to play a major part in the development of new technology for a whole range of instruments including submarine cable fault locators, medical electronics and electrical standards and will no doubt continue to develop its role of satisfying the exacting needs of industry throughout the world.

As Lord Kelvin had observed 'When you cannot measure it, when you cannot express it in numbers, your knowledge is of a meagre and unsatisfactory kind.' Henry Tinsley and his successors have ensured that our knowledge of electricity did not remain meagre and unsatisfactory for long. This extraordinary company which grew from humble beginnings in a garden shed now rightly enjoys its well earned global reputation.

Top left: An interior view of the factory, 2001.
Below: The present management; Mr R A Domoney, Managing Director (left) and Mr N L Dow, Finance Director (right). Mr Domoney joined Tinsley in 1958 as an Apprentice Instrument Maker; is a Freeman of the City of London, and a Liveryman in the Worshipful Company of Scientific Instrument Makers. Mr Dow joined the company in 1988 and is a Fellow of the Institute of Chartered Accountants.

Tinsley's has the advantage of being far more flexible than larger organisations being able to respond very quickly if it feels that changes or modifications in the design of its instruments is required.

Fortunately almost all Tinsley instruments are built in small batches, typically five or ten at a time. Many of the firm's employees have worked with the business for many years and have an in depth knowledge of the business and customers' needs whether it be refurbishing the old or developing new products entirely.

One of the outstanding achievements of recent years is Tinsley's range of Submarine Cable Test equipment which has been produced to detect faults in, and locate, submarine cables. It is used by virtually all the major cable manufacturers and telecommunication companies throughout the world. The demand for Tinsley's equipment is increasing rapidly as the use of fibre-optics and the growth of the Internet creates new demands for new products to serve the telecommunications industry.

Now, in a new century, as it has since its birth, 'Tinsley's' is still producing high precision, state-of-the-art equipment which is sold to a wide variety of industrial users as well as calibration laboratories and national laboratories including the NPL where our National Standards are maintained. In recent years Tinsley has also moved into the medical instrumentation business becoming the number one supplier of visual field analysers sold to opticians and eye hospitals throughout the United Kingdom.

Today Tinsley is still a small company, but it is one with a very big reputation and one whose name is synonymous with quality and reliability. The

Halls of fame

The Fairfield Halls in Park Lane were built in 1962 by the County Borough of Croydon to create a centre in South London for entertainment and the arts.

The final decision to build Fairfield was made by Croydon Council in July 1955. It would mean that Croydon's rich theatrical tradition could continue despite the loss of the Grand and Davis Theatres in the town's redevelopment plan.

£1,250,000 had eventually to be found to meet the cost of building which was designed by architects Robert Atkinson & Partners and was built by Holloway Bros. Ltd.

The 'fair field' on which the building stands was, for five and a half centuries, the scene of the ancient Croydon Fair. In 1314 King Edward II granted to the Archbishop of Canterbury the right to hold an annual fair in his Manor of Croydon which, save for the interruptions of war and pestilence, was to be held every year until 1866 on 'the Vigil and Morrow of the Feast of Saint Matthew'. Originally, and for centuries thereafter, Croydon Fair was a trading fair and perhaps a hiring fair too where sheep, cattle and corn were sold and where maidservants and farm labourers were hired. Gradually it changed to become a pleasure fair and by the 1850s had become notorious for its rowdy customers who, as rowdy customers usually do, came from outside Croydon to make a nuisance of themselves in the town. Eventually in 1866 Croydon Fair was suppressed to the accompaniment of some lively rioting in which visitors to Croydon repaid the town's hospitality by breaking some of the most respected heads in the town.

In 1866 what was then known as The Fairfield was bought by the Brighton Railway Company and as recently as 1933 the ground was still being used for sidings and workshops by the Southern Railway Company. Alerted by a plan to build a greyhound racing track on Fairfield the Croydon Corporation bought this ancient

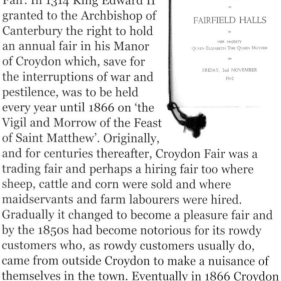

Above left: *Fairfield Halls under construction.*
Above right: *The programme from the opening night in November 1962.*
Left: *Fairfield Halls in the early 1960s.*

purchase of the surrounding roads and land.

In December 1958 the Council gave its approval to go ahead with the scheme. Since the idea had been first proposed the estimated cost had, by 1959, risen to £750,000.

The building would consist of three main units: the Fairfield Concert Hall, the Ashcroft Theatre and the Arnhem Gallery with shared Foyer, Box Office and Catering facilities. Spacious licensed bars were available whilst the Foyer Buffet would be open from 10.30am each day. Thinking of the future the development would also provide more than 1,400 carpark spaces in underground and multi storey carparks.

Top left and right: *The magnificent organ in the Concert Hall.* ***Above right:*** *An aerial view of Croydon from 1959.* ***Below:*** *An aerial view of Croydon dated 1962, showing the Fairfield Halls on the far right.*

site in 1934. Much of the original Fair Field would eventually be occupied by the then Croydon College of Design and Technology, but it is pleasant to think that Fairfield Halls though a far cry from the fit-up theatres, the mountebanks and thimble-riggers of Croydon Fair continues the traditional use of the field for the pleasure and entertainment of Croydon people.

It was T Arthur Lewis, chairman of the Town Planning & Improvements Committee in 1933, who had really set the ball rolling and by 1938 a proposal to build a new civic centre and concert halls was mooted at a cost of £165,000. Designs were invited and a prize of £500 awarded for the best plan. That May however, amidst much controversy, a post card referendum was held and rate payers voted against the huge expenditure. It hardly mattered: in September the country was at war with Germany and all bets were off. It was not to be until July 1955 that the Finance Committee would reopen the now dusty file for the project which would ultimately require a Parliamentary Bill to facilitate the compulsory

The concert hall was formally named the Fairfield Hall by Queen Elizabeth the Queen Mother at the opening ceremony held on Friday 2nd November 1962. An inaugural concert was given by the BBC Symphony Orchestra conducted by the late Sir Malcolm Sargent and featuring Yehudi Menuhin as soloist. Planned primarily for concerts the hall had a raked floor and fixed seating but was easily adapted for open stage performances, arena events and films. The concert hall was described by Leopold Stokowski as 'the perfect Symphony Hall' and was soon being regularly visited by top national and international orchestras and soloists. It also played host to the very best of pop, rock and comedy as well as jazz, films, folk, sports and children's events.

One feature is the Royal Box; it is rarely used by the Royal Family, not least because of its poor view - it is primarily designed for the audience to see them. It was perhaps significant that the Queen Mother chose not to sit there for the inaugural concert although it was used in 1983 when Queen Elizabeth II attended a concert in June 1983 to celebrate the centenary of Croydon being granted its charter in 1883.

Seating capacity including choir and boxes was 1,794 but for recitals by small groups and solo artists this could be increased by the addition of 136 seats on the orchestra tiering. The Upper Stalls could be closed off by a fibre-glass curtain, although the high attendance figures enjoyed in the Concert Hall lead to that facility being used only

Top: *Segovia in the Concert Hall.*
Above left: *A poster advertising a run of No Bed for Bacon by Carol Brahms and Ned Sherrin in the Ashcroft Theatre.* ***Above right:*** *A programme for a Variety Show in the 1960s.*

rarely.

The underside of each seat had holes drilled in it, these were acoustically designed so that each seat absorbed an equal amount of sound whether it is occupied or empty. As a result a concert will sound the same even if the Hall is only half full.

The platform was formed by 15 sections on lifts and could be lowered to auditorium floor level thus making the Hall suitable for arena events or tiered as required. The front three sections could be lowered below floor level to create an orchestra pit.

A projection room at the rear of the balcony coupled with a large roll-up screen gave full size Cinemascope facilities which were augmented in 1985 by the installation of completely new sound equipment.

An organ was installed at a cost of £23,000 designed by Ralph Downes and constructed by Harrison & Harrison Ltd. The organ was situated to one side of the orchestra and when not in use the organ console was housed out of sight beneath the choir seating. Refurbishing the organ many years later would cost

£48,000!

The Ashcroft Theatre was named after the Croydon-born actress Dame Peggy Ashcroft. She spoke a

prologue written by Sir John Betjeman before the first performance on 5th November 1962 of the now long-forgotten play by Herman Gressieker 'Royal Gambit' concerning Henry VIII and his six wives and starring Michael Dennison and Dulcie Gray which had only recently been translated from its original German.

When the Ashcroft opened the Pembroke Theatre Company whose theatre in Wellesley Road was being demolished to make way for an office block moved into the Ashcroft as resident company; they performed many famous productions before moving on again in 1967.

More than ten years after the Ashcroft Theatre opened Dame Peggy made her first professional appearance at the Theatre starring in a Harold Pinter double bill presented by the Royal Shakespeare Company. The event was part of the first Croydon Arts Festival which was held from 21st to the 28th April 1973 and centred on the Fairfield Halls; appropriately the programme included the Royal Philharmonic Orchestra giving the first performance of a new work by Malcolm Arnold - 'Concert Overture: The Fair Field'.

The Ashcroft Theatre soon enjoyed an unrivalled reputation for out-of-town attractions including pre-West End plays, touring productions, pantomimes and repertory. It was also frequently used by amateur societies.

For the technically minded this is a proscenium theatre with a stepped auditorium

Top right: *The ornately decorated safety curtain in the Ashcroft Theatre.*
Left, both pictures: *Scenery in various stages of production.*

providing 734 seats, 216 of which are in the circle. There are particularly good sight lines from all seats and owing to the fine acoustics audibility is excellent.

The stage apron was mounted on an electrically operated lift and could be used to create an orchestra pit or be raised to provide an extension to the stage.

The stage itself had 30 counter weighted stage lines and a generous fly gallery. A large scene dock had high access doors to the stage and to the loading bay in the theatre yard whilst a comprehensive range of lighting and equipment could be provided.

Not every event however is suited to a concert hall or theatre. For exhibitions, displays and conferences, children's entertainments, banquets and dances, beauty contests and fashion shows the Arnhem Gallery was the perfect venue: 88ft long and 55ft wide it had a wall display area of 6,000 square feet. The name reflects the links which have long

Above: The impressive entrance.
Below: The entrance foyer in the early 1960s.

existed between the towns of Croydon and Arnhem. The town in Holland was famed during the closing stages of the second world war for being the centre of 'Operation Market Garden' later filmed as a 'A Bridge Too Far' in which Allied paratroops and airborne forces heroically, if unsuccessfully, attempted to capture and hold the bridge at Arnhem far ahead of the advancing Allied front line.

The Arnhem Gallery was originally provided with a glass roof to let in as much light as possible; the design was subsequently found to be flawed making the gallery too hot in summer and too cold in winter. Today the full extent of the original roof can only be seen from outside.

The Gallery could be divided in two by a folding wooden screen. Other facilities included a portable catwalk for fashion parades and a mobile band platform with a musicians gallery at the first floor level. The maple floor provided an excellent dancing surface and the adjacent kitchen ensured quick service at dinner dances and banquets when up to 400 people could be catered for. The Arnhem Gallery was complemented

could get one a seat to watch Mick McManus and Les Kellett engaging in a bout of all in wrestling, or for 5 shillings see Norman Vaughan in an all star variety show or Acker Bilk's Jazzband, the legendary Duke Ellington and his orchestra as well as Freddy and the Dreamers or Dusty Springfield.

by the Arnhem Reception Bar itself 55ft by 24ft which could be open to the main gallery if required whilst on the second floor the Maple Room proved ideal accommodation for wedding receptions, lunches and dinners or business meetings for up to 100 people.

Curiously one feature omitted by the designers was office space; two flats were provided for the manager and the caretaker; these were later to be converted into offices - and an extra level of offices was constructed above these in 1989. A further modification was made to the shared Green Room used by both the Ashcroft and Concert hall; the location proved to be impractical and it was subsequently converted into the Green Room Restaurant.

Perhaps one of the most interesting elements of the Fairfield Halls organisation was the idea of Tom Pyper the first General Manager who recruited a voluntary and unpaid corps of stewards and programme sellers. A team of ladies would sell programmes at all performances whilst gentlemen would welcome patrons to the halls and conduct them to their seats. During the weeks prior to the opening no fewer than 210 men and 60 women volunteered. They came from all walks of life: bankers, milkmen, secretaries and civil servants - there was even a retired British Ambassador all united in the belief that the Fairfield Halls were a credit to their town.

Since its opening so many years ago Fairfield has been host to many millions of visitors. Readers who are natives of Croydon will inevitably have many happy memories of visiting the Fairfield Halls which have catered for every possible taste: highbrow plays and musical recitals may have appealed to many but for others far more entertaining fare would be offered during that first year when 3 shillings and sixpence

Much has changed over the years however: technology has moved on and the nature and types of show have evolved. Fairfield is reviewing the needs of its customers and performers. A major refurbishment is programmed and some of the world's leading consultants have been drafted in to come up with the Fairfield of the future.

The Concert Hall with the finest orchestral acoustic in Europe will not be changed, the Ashcroft Theatre however needs to become more versatile and have the ability to stage bigger theatrical shows. The public areas will be also be improved to ensure better customer flow and improved catering facilities.

Fairfield of today intends to ensure that its future will reflect and match all the glory of its distinguished past.

Above left: *The Arnhem Gallery decked out for a wedding.* ***Above right:*** *HRH The Queen Mother on the opening night of Fairfield Halls, NOVEMBER 1962.* ***Below:*** *A concert being televised in the Concert Hall.*

Keeping it traditional, making it innovative

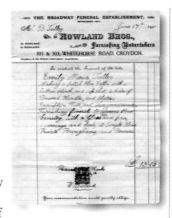

Rowland Brothers have been serving the communities in Croydon since 1875. Originally based in Whitehorse Road, West Croydon, they recently developed another premises at 44 High Street, Purley to improve their service in the south of the Borough.

These new premises were designed to offer modern facilities and provide a suitable base for the comprehensive funeral services to which the residents of Croydon and Purley are accustomed. Included in the complex are five chapels of various denominations, refrigeration facilities, a coffin showroom, two arranging offices and comfortable reception facilities. The premises provide easy access for the elderly and disabled.

This is very different from their original premises in which the great grandfather of the present partners started out but while the buildings may be different, the deceased is now transported by a traditional fleet of luxury cars. A copy invoice in the company archives gives the details of funeral arrangements carried out in June 1921, which included a polished Elm coffin with four pairs of brassed handles and plate, transporting the coffin to Queen's Road cemetery in a glass carriage with a pair of horses for the sum of £13/10/0. The same funeral arrangements at today's prices would cost close to £3,000.00. Details may change but the attitude of care and professionalism remains just as it always has been.

The Rowland Brothers, Tony, David, Bob and

Above left: *An invoice dated 1921.* ***Right:*** *The firm's original premises on Whitehorse Road.* ***Below:*** *A fine turnout in the early 1900s.*

sister Jacki and their children Stephen, Melanie, Andrew and Paul are proud to carry on the long family tradition of care for all aspects of the funeral process, and in addition are keen to develop their expertise to respond to changing needs of recent times. When deaths of holiday-makers are reported in the press little coverage is given to the arrangements which need to be made for returning the bodies home. Rowland Brothers have been providing advice and international repatriation services of a high standard for over thirty years. In fact such are their reputation and expertise that they have recently become official advisors in this area to The National Association of Funeral Directors.

Consulates, Embassies and Government Departments world-wide rely on Rowland Brothers to find a way through the huge logistical difficulties involved in bringing a body home. In addition, through their bereavement service, they provide face-to-face support and advice to bereaved relatives anywhere in the world. The value to distressed relatives, who may not speak the local language, of having competent and compassionate support at this difficult time cannot be

Top: A funeral cortege in the 1950s. **Above:** *An early advertisement for W Rowland & Sons.*

overestimated. The firm is connected to a global network of over 800 funeral directors who each have an excellent reputation, providing high quality, professional services to their local communities.

They are able to balance care and exceptional service and cost management, which has given Rowland Brothers International a particularly high reputation when acting for insurance and assistance companies. Thousands of pounds can be saved simply by getting it right, but in the world of international repatriation nothing is simple or straightforward.

This global service started when they were asked to exhume a French Countess in England for repatriation to France and has earned them a number of '1st's'. They were the first company to have a hearse carried by Hovercraft. They also introduced embalming services to the Gambia - Tony Rowland took it upon himself to teach one of the doctors in a hospital in Banjul.

An important part of the Rowland tradition has been their standing as high quality stonemasons and the brothers were honoured to be entrusted with the commission to supply the Kenley War Memorial. The 18ft long and 7ft high Portland stone carving commemorates those who served at the Kenley Aerodrome between 1917 and 1958. The memorial depicts a pilot flanked by representatives of ground crew of both sexes and has a record of all the operational squadrons that were based at Kenley.

It was unveiled on August 19, 1999 at a ceremony to commemorate the Battle of Britain sixty years before, in which, at Kenley alone, 80 aircraft were lost and 32 airmen killed, part of those designated by Winston Churchill as 'The Few'. Crews from Croydon, Kenley, Redhill, Fairoaks, Biggin Hill, Gatwick, Brooklands and Dunsfold, took Hawker Hurricanes and Vickers Supermarine Spitfires to repel Messerschmitts, Dorniers, Heinkels and Junkers on that occasion. About five thousand people turned out to witness this unveiling and the RAF Battle of Britain Memorial Flight, of a Lancaster, a Spitfire and a Hurricane honoured the gathering with fly-past. Also present to pay their respects were representatives from America, Australia, Canada and Poland whose pilots had also served at the aerodrome during World War Two.

Rowland Brothers also supplied the new memorial stone on the grave of the legendary Secretary of the Football Association from 1870-1895, Charles Alcock who 'invented' the FA Cup and began the process which has seen football become an

international sport. For years his grave was marked by just a number - but grandees from the Football Association and Surrey County Cricket Club (which he also served as Secretary from 1872-1907) gathered at West Norwood cemetery for the re-dedication. Geoff Thompson, Chairman of the Football Association at the time gave an address in which he expressed thanks on behalf of thousands of players and hundreds of millions of spectators who have watched the FA Cup through the years, to Alcock for his vision and achievement, and his hope that there would be other people who could do similarly great things for football in the future. He also said that it is frequently asserted that football matches between international teams are today's peaceful re-enactments of the battles, which used to be fought between armies - if this is true then Alcock's contribution to world peace is considerable. The memorial stone, made of marble, features a striking cross on which a replica of the FA Cup has been carved. The grave also contains other members of his family. Attempts were made to trace living relatives but none were found to represent the family at the rededication service.

Top right: *A funeral from the 1990s.* ***Above:*** *Left to right: Bob, Tony, David and the late Jim Rowland.* ***Left:*** *One of the Chapels of Rest.*

Golden Leaves (Rowland Brothers established the company in 1984) provides funeral-planning services throughout the UK and other countries in Europe. Funeral plans offer a sensible and secure way to relieve your loved ones and executors of the difficulties often encountered when arranging and financing a funeral. It is not an insurance policy and requires no medical.

Rowland Brothers has recently become a green company, in partnership with the Future Forests environmental task force. The carbon emissions of the company assessed (including car mileage, office waste, rates, light and heating, etc.) by the Edinburgh University, Rowland Brothers then plant trees to offset these carbon emissions, effectively making them a carbon neutral company. Golden Leaves, (Rowland Brothers sister company) has created the opportunity for everyone to become 'carbon neutral' by developing and offering a special scheme permitting individuals to offset their household carbon dioxide emissions.

Golden Leaves has also pledged to plant one tree for every existing and future Golden Leaves pre-paid funeral plan holder, as well as to plant enough trees to neutralise any carbon dioxide emissions created by their business on an on-going basis. An initial 1,100 Golden Leaves trees are being planted in the Whitehorse Wood in Kent and more will be planted in time throughout the country.

The Rowland Family are delighted to be contributing towards this scheme which will help to protect the environment at the most fundamental level - the air we breathe and they look forward to seeing the trees planted today growing into a beautiful forest in the years to come.

The scheme is now offered by a network of funeral directors throughout the UK. There are also offices in Spain, the Algarve, Malta and Cyprus where there is a significant expatriate community. Golden Leaves is the only funeral planning company to provide a repatriation plan for British expatriates living abroad and for foreign expatriates living in the UK.

The Rowland family has been serving the residents of Croydon with empathy for over 125 years, offering a professional, yet caring, service maintaining traditional standards, whilst constantly seeking to identify and meet changing needs.

Top left: *the dedication ceremony for the memorial to the aircrew and ground staff who worked at Kenley Aerodrome between 1917 and 1954.* ***Top right:*** *The unveiled memorial.* ***Above left:*** *the memorial stone on the grave of Charles Alcock.* ***Below:*** *Steve and Tony Rowland with Dan Morell of Future Forests planting trees in the Whitehorse Wood in Kent.*

Family gets down to brass tacks

All residents of Croydon must be familiar with 'Turtles' as it is universally known. In fact quite a number of them not only remain loyal to them despite the presence of the larger national DIY chains but actually prefer the service and range of goods offered by the family firm. In 1995 the firm was awarded the Retail Courtesy Award given by the Croydon Guardian after nominations were invited from readers. Many grateful customers were able to express their appreciation to the Turtles staff for their knowledge and friendliness.

The staff still wear traditional ironmongers' overalls and many of the 40 or so sales force are themselves retired engineers, carpenters, woodworkers and electricians. Their advice is free and expert. Between them they have decades of DIY experience and are happy and able to give advice to those with less specialised know-how.

The award represented a recognition of the contribution the firm has made to the people of Croydon for over a hundred years, during which time it has been continually in the hands of family members.

The business began in a small way at 6 Crown Hill when Louis Henry Turtle purchased the tool

and cutlery shop which had been started in the 1880s by Thomas Lindley. Turtle's background had been as a travelling salesman for a firm of manufacturing cutlers in Sheffield. His travels took him far and wide including to Ireland twice every year. Perhaps long absences away from home became less congenial after his marriage in 1883 and this is what led him to decide to go into the retail trade. He came across the Crown Hill shop on his travels and bought the business in 1894. At first he rented the property but subsequently acquired the freehold. Henry and his family lived above the shop to begin with but gradually the business encroached on all available space and by degrees even the garden

Top left: Company founder, Louis Henry Turtle. ***Above right:*** *The shop in the early 1900s.* ***Right:*** *An early delivery vehicle at the start of the 20th century.*

been casting an eagle eye over the quality and range of tools available in the New World.

It was in 1964 that the decisive move to new premises in Park Street was made and Turtle's introduced what must have been one of the country's first self-service DIY shops. They were later to construct their own warehouse and headquarters.

Specialist in tools, machinery and accessories for wood-working and engineering, Turtle's supply almost everything connected with ironmongery, plumbing, home DIY, gardening, household goods and arts and crafts. They take great pride in being able to supply screws to a customer's required quantity and not in prepacked amounts. They offer a free home delivery service within the Croydon area for larger items. Though the vast majority of customers come from the Croydon area, Turtle's customer base is far more widely spread. They advertise in nationally distributed journals on woodworking and have exhibited in the Practical Woodworking Exhibition in Wembley.

Many items are stocked which are not normally available elsewhere as Turtles refuse to stock their shelves purely on the basis of expected turnover and they pride themselves on carrying a range of items which justifies the opinion expressed by many Croydonians, 'No doubt, I can get it at Turtle's'.

Top left: An early tram advertising Turtle's wares.
Above right: An early advertisement for the shop.
Below: The modern shop front at the start of a new millennium.

was built over. The company occupied this site until early 1964.

Louis Henry's shop was considered an 'Aladdin's cave' just as the store is today. He sold model trains and steam engines, firearms and Meccano construction sets were stocked as well as spectacles which Louis dispensed himself until stricter regulations stipulated that only qualified practitioners should be allowed to do so. He also stocked wireless sets and offered an accumulator charging service - a line which was discontinued when the technology became infinitely more complex. The foundation of his business was tools and cutlery and apart from selling new items, he also offered a top-notch tool repair service overseen by Sheffield-trained craftsmen.

Louis Turtle also played his part in the wider commercial life of the town. He was President for the 1912/13 period of the Croydon Chamber and ventured to the USA on a Chamber sponsored mission in the early 1900s. Whatever his wider instructions and concerns on that occasion may have been, it is beyond doubt that he would have

Adams family values

It's a fact of life that building firms come and go. Most survive a few years or decades then simply disappear. Others, by contrast, a happy few who seem to have got the formula right, continue trading indefinitely despite the economic ups and downs which periodically convulse the building industry. Even so it is rare to find a firm which has been in business for more than fifty years.

Croydon's Adams Bros. building company based in Croham Road began trading in 1946, following the end of the second war. It was a good time to start work in the building industry; thanks to the attentions of Herr Hitler and the Luftwaffe vast swathes of England's towns and cities had been reduced to rubble. Even those properties which had survived bombing intact had either suffered minor damage which needed repairing or, due to the shortage of workmen, caused by them being called up for the

Above: Inserting a time capsule at the Roman Catholic Church, Tadworth, Surrey. Below: Building the Reception Centre for handicapped persons in the London Borough of Sutton.

armed forces, had not been subject to normal maintenance since the outbreak of war in 1939.

As the name suggests the firm of Adams Bros. was founded by three brothers Edward, Robert and George Adams after they were demobbed from the forces.

Edward and George Adams, carpenters and joiners, were very fine tradesmen, highly skilled and self disciplined. It was however their brother Robert, an academic with no trade skills and as a result pushed into the office by his brothers, who strove to move the firm forwards, looking to expand business at every opportunity.

Being a devoted Catholic Robert secured contracts to build several new churches and halls. There were sometimes perks to those jobs: when working on a church through the winter period the grateful priest fortified the workers with altar wine.

At the outset the brothers had no previous business experience but just went looking for work from their base at Edward Adams's house in Chislehurst. After

service and quality were the key to success. This was important because although there was a plethora of work after the war the firm needed to establish a name for itself in competition with many other similar businesses.

Adams Brothers continues trying to give the best service and build quality possible. A major factor in this has been the loyalty of the firm's staff. In 1948 when the firm was established it was the norm for building contractors to employ direct labour, since then more and more firms have moved away from that idea for economic reasons; Adams Bros. however has always considered employing its own staff to be an important factor in its delivery of a quality of service.

That policy has paid off. Over the decades the Adams Bros business has survived where many others have fallen by the wayside. There may no longer be war damage to repair but today's clients, mainly local authorities and commercial institutions, have no difficulty recognising quality.

Today a second generation of the Adams family is now taking the firm and its values forward into the 21st century.

initially concentrating on war damage repair work the brothers gradually expanded their new business to execute medium-sized building contracts.

The firm became a limited company in September 1948. It was a good time to be alive: not only had the war ended but there was an air of optimism around; life was starting again, the baby boom generation was being born and the Labour government had implemented changes which promises a utopian future as earlier that year coal, steel and the railways had been nationalised, India was granted independence and the NHS and the welfare state promised security for all.

In that climate of business confidence it was possible to believe that anything was possible. Around 1950, full of faith in the future the Adams brothers moved to new premises in Magdela Road, South Croydon where the firm would remain for over forty years before moving to Croham Road in 1995.

Edward and George Adams eventually left the firm leaving Robert to run the business the way he wanted. Robert may have run the business on his own but the philosophy which he and his two brothers set out with would remain: the idea that

Top left: *An interior reception centre, Sutton.*
Above left: *Interior of St Aidan's Church, Coulston.* ***Below:*** *The formation of a maze in the Elizabethan Garden at Whitgift School, Croydon.*

Patently trading on their marks of success

Three stripes on a sweatshirt sleeve, the word 'Coke,' the name 'Dyson' these all conjure up certain very particular associations in the minds of millions of people and this is far from being an accident. The process by which this takes place is one of the many areas of expertise belonging to the patent agent.

Lone inventors and massive multinational companies have benefited from the services of Raworth, Moss & Cook in the complex world of patents, trade marks, designs and copyright for over a hundred years.

Founded in 1894 it is one of the UK's leading and oldest-established intellectual property law firms. It is a partnership of European Patent Attorneys, UK Chartered Patent Attorneys, European Trade Mark Attorneys and UK Registered Trade Mark Attorneys. They deal with all aspects of intellectual property from initial advice, filing applications for patents, trade marks and designs through to

Above: The auctioneers notice of sale of The Lindens in 1921, now Raworth House. **Right:** *An artist's impression of Raworth House.* **Below:** *Mr James Moss, one of the early partners in the firm.*

the defence of the rights obtained in this way and attacking the rights of third parties where appropriate, not only in the UK but throughout the world.

The origin of the firm can be traced back to a practice started by Newham Browne in London. When he died in 1905, John Ernest Raworth took over the clients when he was just 29. At this time Raworth's offices were in 73 Cheapside, London EC2 and later at 28 Broadway, London SW1. In 1919 he took Ernest Moss into partnership, who at offices in Victoria Street made all the staff line up at the windows and cheer whenever members of the Royal Family went past; he was particularly proud of his membership of The Dynamicables, an exclusive London dining club of electrical engineers. John Cook, a New Zealander, was associated with the firm for a relatively short time, as he died from heart

An auction Bill of 1921 records that this 'substantially built double-fronted detached freehold residence...front garden with carriage sweep and good garden in the rear'; was then known as The Lindens; a significant feature at the time was that '...electric light is installed, water laid on and the drains connected with the sewer'! It was let on lease to His Majesty's Postmaster-General at an annual rent of just £55, but subsequently purchased by the practice. However, though internal alterations have been necessary to meet the demands of a modern professional operation, the exterior remains virtually unchanged since it was built. The Auction Bill claimed that it was 'conveniently situated within eight minute's walk of East and West Croydon Stations', they have checked- it still is.

Today they have clients in virtually every country of the world, with special emphasis on North America, the Far and Middle East and Europe, they offer to them all a personal friendly service combined with the expertise of highly trained specialist staff and modern equipment.

Top left: The staff in 1994, Raworth's Centenary Year. Above left: B Fisher's certificate electing him as a Fellow of the Chartered Institute of Patent Agents in 1955. Below left: Graham Feakins, Partner. Below right: Stephen J Wise, Partner.

failure when he was only 53. Nevertheless he brought a wealth of experience to the firm. Two other significant figures in the firm's history were James Henry Moss, no relation to Ernest William, who made a very large contribution to the technical quality of the practice and was a great patent agent, and the other was Bernard Fisher who established the committee which bore his name which sought to persuade the Chartered Institute of Patent Agents to move actively towards the harmonisation of British and European Patent Law.

Offering high standards of expertise to present day clients are the current partners, Stephen Wise who manages the Trade Mark department and specialises in chemistry, chemical engineering, biotechnology and all aspects of trade marks and Graham Feakins whose area of special expertise is patent litigation, mechanical and civil engineering, design protection and copyright.

It is a fundamental tenet of good working practice that the environment in which it takes place reflects the philosophy of the practice. The firm has the great advantage of being based at Raworth House, a spacious early Victorian mansion which they have enjoyed since 1970.

Building on the past

ow many small building firms have been created in the last fifty or sixty years we wonder? Many thousands each year one would guess, but with almost as many disappearing in the same period. The building trade is a notoriously fickle industry being particularly vulnerable to the vagaries of the national economy. But not every modestly sized building business is short-lived.

The well known local firms of Fortidec Ltd and its sister business Pools Contractors both based at Progress House in Frant Road, Thornton Heath began life in 1947 with the birth of the Pools business shortly followed, in 1952, by Fortidec.

The founders were Charles Pool and Reg W Logan who had previously worked in plastering and the import and export trade respectively. Now they branched out, Charles managing the firm's staff and Reg as the Company Secretary and Accountant.

From the outset the original businesses involved plastering, fibrous mouldings, flooring finishes such as granite and screed as well as small building works and decorations, plumbing and drainage works. Fortidec specialised in meeting clients

demands for long delayed repairs and redecoration after war damage.

Plaster, cement, lime, sand and mortar were all stored at Frant Road in addition to building materials salvaged from war damaged properties kept alongside such limited new materials as were permitted for registered companies operating in those austere post-war times.

The period which followed the second world war was undoubtedly a strange one to modern eyes: because of shortages only registered companies were issued certificates by the government to allow contractors to work and to obtain materials and fuel. And such companies had to handle every aspect of building repairs from drains to roofs and decorations.

The eventual ending of post war rationing did not however mean things would always proceed smoothly: certainly Mr Macmillan might tell us that we'd never had it so good but the firm would still have to suffer later plaster shortages, fuel

Below: *Founder members and staff attending association dinner dance.*

shortages, and even a copper tubing famine in 1971 as well as enduring periods of labour shortages.

Back in 1947 however the businesses were being run from Walpole Mews, Colliers Wood with a yard and storage area in Frant Road. In 1960 the Frant Road yard was redeveloped for office space in the first stage of the company's development. Today the site also contains gas heating and hot water equipment for all types of installations, radiators, copper tubing, electrical and system controls.

A second stage of building began at Frant Road in 1982 to produce the present Progress House.

Today main customers are local authorities, housing associations, public buildings, surveyors and private markets; manufacturers also pass on jobs. Fortidec's largest client is Croydon Council whilst Pools' finds most of its work for surveying practices covering London and the home counties. The main services provided are the planned maintenance of gas appliances as well as repair contracts for local authorities and housing associations along with building works, repairs and decorations. Together the two companies cover all aspects of building, maintenance and repairs and gas servicing for 24 hours a day on 365 days per year providing a dedicated service for their clients.

The companies aim to provide an ever improving service by providing the best labour and materials possible and continuously retraining their staff. Both companies aim to move with

the times in order to continually provide the latest technology. Staff are highly trained and well motivated with a fully trained, computer-literate office staff operating a computerised office system and data base. Directors of the companies are in contact with external staff on a day to day basis ensuring that the company retains its personal friendly approach on all fronts.

In the future the companies intend to continue to expand year on year and continue to ensure that their labour force is retrained regularly. All mobile units are modern, staff are given mobile communications to improve working; and the company is making preparations to upgrade its computer system to enable e-trading.

Now with a second generation of the family involved in the businesses they still agree with the founders' opinion that care and reliability should be the hallmark of specialist contractors.

To find two firms which have survived since the 1950s in such an unforgiving industry is almost unique - the founders' philosophy clearly works.

Above, both pictures: A fleet of equipped vehicles in their new livery. ***Below:*** The present management team.

Shopping - the heart of Croydon

No town today can consider itself complete without a large modern shopping centre. The Drummond Centre in the heart of Croydon was opened on 4th July 1985 and continues to develop into what will eventually be 75,000 square metres of shopping space. The official opening however took place the following year, on Saturday May 17th; the ceremony being presided over by Michelle and Lofty from Eastenders television series when over half a million people visited the centre.

Below: *An aerial view of the Drummond Shopping Centre.*

The modern shopping centre is part of the St Martins Property Group whose own history goes back to 1924; the history of shopping on the site of the Drummond Centre however goes back to 1853 when William Kennard opened a shop there which was to grow to a size previously unprecedented south of the Thames.

Kennard's shop started as just 7 and 8 North End before in 1886 adding numbers 15 and 17, numbers 11 and 13 were added to the store ten years later, number 23 in 1907 and finally numbers 25 to 31 in 1911.

Kennard's of Croydon's 'Wonder store of the South' or a 'Town within a Store' became

The centre was refurbished over an eight month period in 1996; the internal stainless steel cladding was replaced by lighter material and natural light introduced into the malls. A section of the mall and fourteen smaller shops were amalgamated to create a new 3000m² TK Maxx and a 700m² Spoils Kitchen Reject Shop. The central café, previously converted from the original fountain, was removed creating a large central atrium in which now stands a 10 metre tall Christmas tree during the festive season.

In early 2001 St Martins had recently started the construction of a brand new 42,000m² shopping centre trading on four levels, adjacent to the Drummond Centre. To make way for the new scheme the centre's 860-space multi-storey car park will be demolished (top right of the aerial view) and an entrance created onto North End, on the site of the former C&A that closed in September 2000.

nationally famous and by 1935 it had grown to occupy a ten acre site employing 1,200 staff and serving 8 million customers a year.

In 1973 Kennard's became part of Debenhams. The site was redeveloped in 1980 by the St Martins Group at a cost of £24.5 million and 'Drummond Place' was opened in May 1986.

Clad in gleaming white aluminium the new shopping centre added a new dimension to south London's premier shopping town featuring three internal 'streets' running through the development converging on a marbled and galleried atrium where fountains played and a scenic glass lift carried shoppers to the upper floors. Architects John Clark Associates, who designed Drummond Place, won the Croydon Design Award for the development.

Drummond Place introduced the concept of covered air-conditioned shopping to Croydon for the first time. Retailers at the time included Debenhams, Gap, Next, Heals, Laura Ashley, Bally, Marks and Spencer Home, Benetton and a Prestos Supermarket. Over a period of time Drummond Place became the Drummond Centre.

A spectacular six-storey curved glazed entrance in Tamworth Road, opposite a new combined tram and bus stop, will become a major gateway to Croydon's retail area. A new 1,000, space multi-storey car park will be built above the centre.

Part of the construction work includes the complete integration of the existing Drummond Centre. The combined centre, ultimately branded as *Centrale*, will house two of the country's most dynamic department stores, Debenhams and the House of Fraser.

Today, residents of Croydon and the surrounding area are ensured that the shopping centre which goes back to William Kennard's first 'superstore' has a bright future.

Above: *North End pictured in the early 1980s prior to its pedestrianisation.*

Residents of Lansdowne Road, Purley celebrate VE Day in style.

Acknowledgments

The publishers wish to thank the following people for their contribution to the book: Stephen Griffiths and his colleagues at Croydon Local Studies Library; Mr John Gent; Mr Malcolm Starbrook, Editor of the Croydon Advertiser Group.

Thanks are also due to
Andrew Mitchell who penned the editorial text,
Steve Ainsworth and Judith Dennis for their copywriting skills